CONTRACT LAW

5th edition

Emily Finch

Stefan Fafinski

Harlow, England • London • New York • Boston • San Francisco • Toronto • Sydney • Auckland • Singapore • Hong Kong
Tokyo • Seoul • Taipei • New Delhi • Cape Town • São Paulo • Mexico City • Madrid • Amsterdam • Munich • Paris • Milan

Pearson Education Limited
Edinburgh Gate
Harlow CM20 2JE
United Kingdom
Tel: +44 (0)1279 623623
Web: www.pearson.com/uk

First published 2008 (print)
Second edition published 2009 (print)
Third edition published 2013 (print and electronic)
Fourth edition published 2015 (print and electronic)
Fifth edition published 2017 (print and electronic)

ISBN: 978-1-292-08686-6 (print)
       978-1-292-08724-5 (PDF)
       978-1-292-08723-8 (ePub)

British Library Cataloguing-in-Publication Data
A catalogue record for the print edition is available from the British Library

10 9 8 7 6 5 4 3 2 1
20 19 18 17 16

Front cover bestseller data from Nielsen BookScan (2009–2014, Law Revision Series).
Back cover poll data from a survey of 16 UK law students in September 2014.

Print edition typeset in 10/12pt Helvetica Neue LT Std by SPi Global
Print edition printed and bound in Malaysia (CTP-PJB)

NOTE THAT ANY PAGE CROSS REFERENCES REFER TO THE PRINT EDITION

Contents

What do you think of LawExpress?

We're really keen to hear your opinions about the series and how well it supports your studies. Your views will help inform the future development of Law Express and ensure it is best suited to the revision needs of law students.

Please log on to the website and leave us your feedback. It will only take a few minutes and your thoughts are invaluable to us.

www.pearsoned.co.uk/lawexpressfeedback

Acknowledgements

This book is dedicated to STG.

We are, as ever, grateful to all who offered feedback on the last edition of *Law Express: Contract Law,* particularly the anonymous academic reviewers who provided some suggestions for improvement. We have been pleased to incorporate these as best we could.

We'd really like to hear what you think of the book, which you can do by visiting www.finchandfafinski.com, Twitter @FinchFafinski or email to hello@finchandfafinski.com.

Emily Finch and Stefan Fafinski

Publisher's acknowledgements

Our thanks go to all reviewers who contributed to the development of this text, including students who participated in research and focus groups which helped to shape the series format.

Introduction

Contract law is one of the core subjects required for a qualifying law degree, so it is a compulsory component of most undergraduate law programmes. It is usually taught as a first- or second-year subject as many of its concepts are relatively straightforward.

This revision guide will help you to identify the relevant law and apply it to factual situations, which should help to overcome preconceived notions of the 'right' outcome in favour of legally accurate assessments of the liability of the parties. The book also provides guidance on the policy underlying the law and it identifies problem areas, both of which will help you to prepare for essay questions. The book is intended to supplement your course materials, lectures and textbooks; it is a guide to revision rather than a substitute for the amount of reading (and thinking) that you need to do in order to succeed.

Contract law is a vast subject – you should realise this from looking at the size of your recommended textbook – so it follows that a revision guide cannot cover all the depth and detail that you need to know and it does not set out to do so. Instead, it aims to provide a concise overall picture of the key areas for revision – reminding you of the headline points to enable you to focus your revision, identify the key principles of law and use these effectively in essays and problem questions.

📖 REVISION NOTE

Things to bear in mind when revising contract law:

- Do use this book to guide you through the revision process.
- Do not use this book to tell you everything that you need to know about contract law but make frequent reference to your recommended textbooks and notes that you have made yourself from lectures and private study.
- Make sure that you consult your syllabus frequently to check which topics are covered and in how much detail.
- Read around the subject as much as possible to ensure that you have sufficient depth of knowledge. Use the suggested reading in this book and on your lecture handouts to help you to select relevant material.

- Take every possible opportunity to practise your essay-writing and problem-solving technique; get as much feedback as you can.

- You should aim to revise as much of the syllabus as possible. Be aware that in contract law many questions that you encounter in coursework and examination papers could combine different topics, e.g. contract formation, misrepresentation and mistake. Therefore, selective revision could leave you unable to answer questions that include reference to material that you have excluded from your revision; it is never a good idea to tackle a question if you are able to deal with only part of the law that is raised.

- Take the time to acquire as many past examination papers from your institution as possible. While this book gives guidance to certain types of questions, you should try to answer previous questions from your own institution. This will ensure that you are familiar with the structure and requirements of your own examination and give you plenty of exposure to the types of question preferred by your own institution.

Before you begin, you can use the study plan available on the companion website to assess how well you know the material in this book and identify the areas where you may want to focus your revision.

Guided tour

How to use features in the book 📖 and on the companion website 🖱

Understand quickly

📖 **Topic maps** – Visual guides highlight key subject areas and facilitate easy navigation through the chapter. Download them from the companion website to pin on your wall or add to your revision notes.

📖 **Key definitions** – Make sure you understand essential legal terms.

📖 **Key cases and key statutes** – Identify and review the important elements of essential cases and statutes you will need to know for your exams.

📖 **Read to impress** – These carefully selected sources will extend your knowledge, deepen your understanding, and earn better marks in coursework and exams.

📖 **Glossary** – Forgotten the meaning of a word? This quick reference covers key definitions and other useful terms.

🖱 **Test your knowledge** – How well do you know each topic? Test yourself with quizzes tailored specifically to each chapter.

🖱 **Podcasts** – Listen as your own personal Law Express tutor guides you through a step-by-step explanation of how to approach a typical but challenging question.

Revise effectively

📖 **Revision checklists** – Identify essential points you should know for your exams. The chapters will help you revise each point to ensure you are fully prepared. Print the checklists from the companion website to track your progress.

📖 **Revision notes** – These boxes highlight related points and areas where your course might adopt a particular approach that you should check with your course tutor.

Study plan – Assess how well you know a subject prior to your revision and determine which areas need the most attention. Take the full assessment or focus on targeted study units.

Flashcards – Test and improve recall of important legal terms, key cases and statutes. Available in both electronic and printable formats.

Take exams with confidence

Sample questions with answer guidelines – Practice makes perfect! Consider how you would answer the question at the start of each chapter then refer to answer guidance at the end of the chapter. Try out additional sample questions online.

Assessment advice – Use this feature to identify how a subject may be examined and how to apply your knowledge effectively.

Make your answer stand out – Impress your examiners with these sources of further thinking and debate.

Exam tips – Feeling the pressure? These boxes indicate how you can improve your exam performance when it really counts.

Don't be tempted to – Spot common pitfalls and avoid losing marks.

You be the marker – Evaluate sample exam answers and understand how and why an examiner awards marks.

Table of cases and statutes

■ Cases

◼ Statutes

▉ Statutory Instruments

▉ European Legislation

Agreement and contractual intention

1

Revision checklist

Essential points you should know:

- [ ] The definitions of offer and acceptance
- [ ] The distinction between an offer, an invitation to treat and a counter offer
- [ ] The rules on communication and withdrawal of offers
- [ ] The rules relating to communication of acceptances
- [ ] The presumptions of legal intent that arise in social, domestic and commercial situations

◼ Topic map

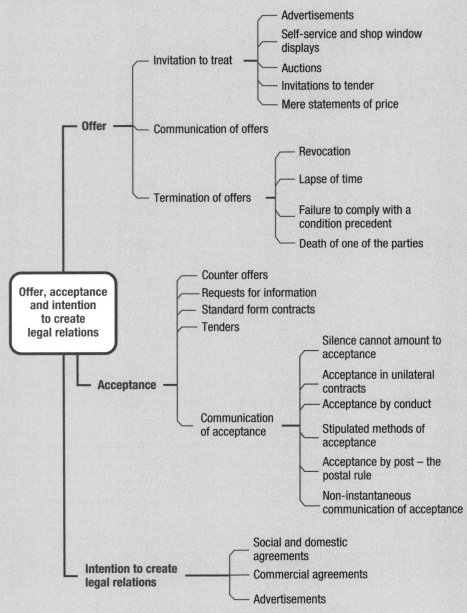

■ Introduction

Offer, acceptance and intention to create legal relations are three of the essential elements in the formation of a valid contract.

This chapter will deal with three of the four composite parts of a binding contract. The final part, consideration, will be covered in Chapter 2. Since a contract is an agreement, it follows that, in order for such an agreement to be reached, there must be an offer made by one party which is accepted by the other. Moreover, to distinguish simple informal agreements from those that are enforced or recognised by law, the parties to the contract must intend to create legal relations between each other.

ASSESSMENT ADVICE

Essay questions

Essay questions on contract formation are uncommon. However, if an essay question does arise, it is likely to cover one specific area of the topic in detail – for instance, whether the postal rule has any place in modern times. These sorts of question require an in-depth focus on specific parts of the material. Since offer, acceptance and intention to create legal relations are an immense topic, essays that consider it as a whole are unlikely.

Problem questions

Problem questions on contract formation are very common. They tend to involve a complex set of facts in which various parties communicate various things to each other by various means and at various times. It is often quite daunting to be faced with a lengthy scenario. However, if you are systematic in your approach, breaking down the facts into a sequence of events and dealing with each issue that comes up in turn, then you should end up with a well-structured argument that should be easier for the marker to follow. Since the vast majority of this topic is governed by case law, it is important to remember to support every legal rule that you put forward in furtherance of your argument by an appropriate and relevant case authority.

Sample question

Could you answer this question? Below is a typical problem question that could arise on this topic. Guidelines on answering the question are included at the end of the chapter, while a sample essay question and guidance on tackling it can be found on the companion website.

PROBLEM QUESTION

On Wednesday, Tom, a vintage car dealer, placed an advertisement in a weekly motor sports magazine offering to sell a Triumph TR6 for £10,000, cheque accepted. Chris saw the advertisement on Thursday and immediately posted a letter to Tom saying that he would be willing to pay £8,000 cash and leaving his work mobile number. On Friday morning, Tom called Chris on his mobile number. Chris did not answer, so Tom left a message which said: 'I'd prefer a cheque for the advertised amount. So the car's yours for that unless I hear back from you to the contrary.' Chris picked up the message and posted a cheque for £10,000. However, at 6.45 p.m. on Friday evening Tom decided not to sell the car to Chris so he called him back on his mobile and left another message. Chris did not use his work mobile over the weekend and had left it in the office which had closed for the weekend when Tom called. Chris did not pick up the new message until early Monday morning. Chris's letter arrived at Tom's address on Saturday but was not opened by him until late Monday morning. On Saturday, Tom sold the car to Sam for £8,000 in cash. Chris now claims that Tom is in breach of contract.

Advise Chris of his legal position.

Offer

An **offer** is an expression of willingness to contract on specified terms, made with the intention that it is to become binding as soon as it is accepted by the person to whom it is addressed.

The party who makes an offer is known as the **offeror**.

The party to whom the offer is addressed is known as the **offeree**.

G.H. Treitel, *The Law of Contract* (Sweet & Maxwell, London, 2003) 8

Originally the courts would determine whether or not an agreement had been reached between the parties by determining whether there had been a meeting of the minds. However, the courts now adopt an *objective* test as to the **offeror**'s intention. Therefore if a reasonable person believed that the alleged offeror implied by his words or conduct that he intended to be bound then this may be sufficient for the **offer** actually to be valid in law, regardless of his actual state of mind. Examples of this include:

- a university which made an unconditional offer of a place to an applicant in error (*Moran* v *University College Salford (No. 2)* [1994] ELR 187);
- a solicitor who mistakenly offered to settle a claim for £150,000 rather than the $155,000 which he had been instructed to offer by his client (*OT Africa Line Ltd* v *Vickers plc* [1996] 1 Lloyd's Rep 700).

An important distinction must be made between an offer and an invitation to treat.

Invitation to treat

KEY DEFINITION: Invitation to treat

An invitation to treat is a preliminary statement expressing a willingness to receive offers.

An **invitation to treat**, therefore, is a statement made by a party inviting offers which that party is then free to accept or reject. An invitation to treat always precedes any offer. This can be illustrated as shown. Figure 1.1 demonstrates the steps in the formation of a simple contract.

Where there is an invitation to treat, this will precede the offer and reverse the parties who make the offer and acceptance (see Figure 1.2).

Although it might seem difficult to distinguish between a genuine offer and a mere invitation to treat since this will depend on the intention of the party making the statement, there are certain situations in which the distinction can be made by applying rules of law. These include:

- advertisements
- self-service and shop window displays
- auctions
- invitations to tender
- mere statements of price.

Figure 1.1

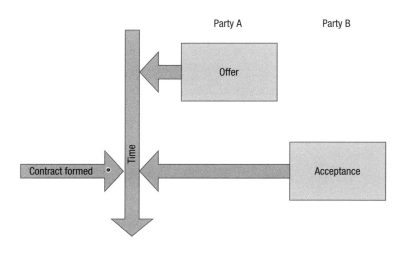

Figure 1.2

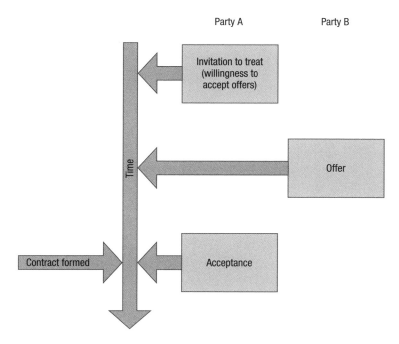

Advertisements

Advertisements are generally considered to be invitations to treat.

KEY CASE

Partridge v *Crittenden* **[1968] 1 WLR 1204**

Concerning: invitation to treat; advertisements

Facts

The defendant placed an advertisement in a magazine stating 'Bramblefinch cocks, bramblefinch hens 25s each.' He was prosecuted under the Protection of Birds Act 1954 for 'offering for sale' wild birds.

Legal principle

The court held that the advertisement was an invitation to treat and not an offer. It was an expression of willingness to receive offers as the starting point of negotiations.

This is also true of catalogues and price lists (*Grainger and Sons* v *Gough* [1896] AC 325).

However, under certain circumstances, an advertisement *may* be regarded as an offer. This will be the case if the advertisement involves a **unilateral offer**.

KEY DEFINITIONS: Unilateral offer; bilateral contract; unilateral contract

A **unilateral offer** is made when one party promises to pay the other a sum of money (or to do some other act) if the other will do something (or forbear from doing so) without making any promise to that effect.

Unilateral contracts (which result from unilateral offers) are distinct from **bilateral contracts** in which a promise is exchanged for a promise. Remember that in a unilateral contract the party to whom the offer is made does not have to promise to do anything in return.

Bilateral contract	Unilateral contract
A promise in return for a promise	A promise in return for an act
Offer and acceptance are both promises	An 'if . . . ' contract–offer is a promise
Both parties are immediately bound (provided there is consideration and intention to create legal relations)	Offeror is bound only if the specific act is performed (provided there is consideration and intention to create legal relations)

Therefore, if an advertisement indicates that the advertiser promises to pay something in return for a particular course of action then the advertiser is bound by that promise. For instance, an advertisement that states '£100 will be paid to anyone who can find my dog, Lassie' is a unilateral offer; however, saying to someone 'I will give you £100 if you find my dog, Lassie' is a bilateral offer which, if accepted, would give rise to a **bilateral contract**. It is the promise that is important here: the fact that it is made in the form of an advertisement (which would normally be regarded as an invitation to treat) is irrelevant.

KEY CASE

Carlill v *Carbolic Smoke Ball Company Ltd* [1893] 1 QB 256

Concerning: unilateral offer; advertisements

Facts

The defendants sold a patent medicine (the 'smoke ball'). They placed a newspaper advertisement stating that they would pay £100 (a very large sum of money in 1893) to anyone who 'contracts the increasing epidemic influenza, colds, or any disease caused by taking cold, after having used the ball three times daily for two weeks according to the printed directions supplied with each ball.' The claimant caught flu after using the ball as directed and claimed the sum of £100. The defendants argued that the advertisement was a 'mere puff' and that, in any case, there was no offer made to any particular person and it was impossible to contract with the whole world.

Legal principle

The Court of Appeal held that the offer in the advertisement was a unilateral offer to the world at large which was accepted by the claimant. This unilateral offer waived the need for communication of acceptance prior to a claim being made on the basis of it. The claimant was therefore entitled to the £100.

The principle from *Carlill* also applies to advertisements offering rewards. These are traditionally treated as offers, rather than as invitations to treat, since there is an intention for the offeror to be bound as soon as the information is given (*Williams* v *Carwardine* (1833) 5 C & P 566).

Self-service and shop window displays

When goods are on display in a self-service shop or in a shop window, their display does not constitute an offer: it is an invitation to treat.

> **KEY CASE**
>
> ***Pharmaceutical Society of Great Britain*** v ***Boots Cash Chemists Ltd*** [1953] **1 All ER 482**
>
> *Concerning: display of goods in a self-service shop; invitation to treat*
>
> **Facts**
>
> The defendants changed the format of their shop from counter service to self-service. Section 18 of the Pharmacy and Poisons Act 1933 provided that the sale of certain drugs should not occur 'other than under the supervision of a registered pharmacist'.
>
> **Legal principle**
>
> The Court of Appeal considered whether the contract was formed at the time that the customer removed the goods from the shelves (not under the supervision of a registered pharmacist) or at the time that the goods were presented at the counter for payment (under the supervision of a registered pharmacist). It was held that the contract was formed when the goods were presented at the cash desk and that the display of goods on the shelf was merely an invitation to treat.

This means that the offer to purchase is made at the cash desk by the purchaser. The shop is then free to accept this offer or reject it. This means that shops are not compelled to sell goods at the price at which they are displayed as the purchaser is offering to buy the item at the stated price at the checkout: the shopkeeper can reject that offer if desired.

The principle from *Boots Cash Chemists* was also applied in a case involving the display of goods in a shop window.

> **KEY CASE**
>
> ***Fisher*** v ***Bell*** [1961] 1 QB 394
>
> *Concerning: display of goods in a shop window; invitation to treat*
>
> **Facts**
>
> A shopkeeper displayed a flick knife in his window. The Offensive Weapons Act 1959 prohibited the 'offering for sale' of various offensive weapons, including flick knives. The shopkeeper was prosecuted under the Act.
>
> **Legal principle**
>
> The prosecution failed. The court held that the display of the knife in the window was an invitation to treat rather than an offer. Therefore, the shopkeeper was not offering it for sale.

Auctions

In a sale at auction, the lot itself (together with the auctioneer's request for bids) is an invitation to treat. Each bid represents an offer to buy the lot at the price offered. Acceptance occurs at the fall of the auctioneer's hammer.

KEY CASE

British Car Auctions v *Wright* **[1972] 1 WLR 1519**

Concerning: auctions; invitation to treat

Facts

The defendants were prosecuted for offering an unroadworthy vehicle for sale. The prosecution failed.

Legal principle

The car had not been offered for sale; there had only been an invitation to treat (bid).

This position is also upheld by section 57(2) of the Sale of Goods Act 1979:

KEY STATUTE

Sale of Goods Act 1979, section 57(2)

A sale by auction is complete when the auctioneer announces its completion by the fall of the hammer, or in other customary manner; and until the announcement is made any bidder may retract his bid.

However, where there is an auction sale 'without reserve' (i.e. there is no minimum price that must be reached before the offer is accepted) then this equates to an offer to sell to the highest bidder which is accepted by the submission of the highest bid. This principle was first stated *obiter* in *Harris* v *Nickerson* (1873) LR 8 QB 266 and was followed by the Court of Appeal in *Barry* v *Davies (t/a Heathcote Ball (Commercial Auctions) & Co)* [2000] 1 WLR 1962.

Invitations to tender

Invitations to tender are normally invitations to treat: therefore the person making the invitation to tender is not bound to accept any of the responses (offers) to the tender (*Spencer* v *Harding* (1870) LR 5 CP 561).

However, if the person making the tender states that he will accept the highest offer to buy goods or the lowest offer for the supply of goods or services, then the tender may be considered to be either an offer or an invitation to submit offers with the undertaking to accept the most favourable, concluding the contract at the time that the best offer is communicated (*Harvela Investments Ltd* v *Royal Trust of Canada (CI) Ltd* [1986] AC 207).

Parties issuing invitations to tender are bound to consider (though not necessarily to accept) a tender properly submitted before any deadline (*Blackpool and Fylde Aero Club* v *Blackpool Borough Council* [1990] 1 WLR 1195).

Mere statements of price

Where a party simply states the minimum price at which they would be willing to sell, this is an invitation to treat rather than an offer.

KEY CASE

Harvey v *Facey* [1893] AC 552

Concerning: statements of price; invitation to treat

Facts

Facey was going to sell his store to Kingston when Harvey and another telegraphed him a message stating 'Will you sell us Bumper Hall Pen? Telegraph lowest cash price – answer paid.'

Facey answered by telegram: 'Lowest price for Bumper Hall Pen £900.'

Harvey answered by telegram: 'We agree to buy Bumper Hall Pen for the sum of nine hundred pounds asked by you.'

Harvey claimed that he had accepted the offer and sued for specific performance of the agreement, and for an injunction to restrain Kingston from taking a conveyance of the property.

Legal principle

There had been no offer. Facey's statement was merely a statement of price and not an offer capable of acceptance.

In a similar case, a local authority wrote to a tenant stating that it may 'be prepared to sell' his council house to him at a stated price together with an application form. The tenant completed the form and returned it to the council. However, a change in council policy meant that the sale did not proceed. The tenant's claim for breach of contract failed, since his completed application form was held to be an offer to buy in response to the council's initial letter which was an invitation to treat (*Gibson* v *Manchester City Council* [1979] 1 WLR 294). It is worth noting, however, that the form of words used can render it sufficiently precise to be an offer capable of acceptance. In *Storer* v *Manchester City Council* [1974] 1 WLR 1403, a case that also involved the sale of a council house, the tenant returned a form headed 'Agreement for Sale'. In this case, the court held that the form had a specific character that made it an offer rather than an invitation to treat, which the tenant had accepted by signing and returning it.

Communication of offers

In order to be valid an offer must be communicated to the **offeree**. This means that no party can be bound by an offer of which they were unaware (*Taylor* v *Laird* (1856) 25 LJ Ex 329). This is true for unilateral as well as bilateral offers: therefore, the offeree must have clear knowledge of the existence of the offer for it to be valid (and thus enforceable) (*Inland Revenue Commissioners* v *Fry* [2001] STC 1715). You have already seen that a unilateral offer can be made to the whole world and may be accepted (by performing the conditions named in it) by anyone who had notice of the offer (*Carlill* v *Carbolic Smoke Ball Co*).

Termination of offers

Offers may cease to exist in a number of ways. Acceptance and express rejection are straightforward situations. If an offer is accepted then a contract is formed (provided that the other elements of the contract – intention to create legal relations and consideration – are present). The offer may simply be refused (in which case there is no contract) or extinguished by a counter offer (see 'Acceptance' later in this chapter). In addition, offers may be terminated by:

- revocation
- lapse of time
- failure to comply with a condition precedent
- death of one of the parties.

Revocation

KEY DEFINITION: Revocation

Revocation refers to the rescinding, annulling or withdrawal of an offer.

Generally speaking, an offer may be withdrawn at any time *prior to acceptance* (*Routledge* v *Grant* (1828) 4 Bing 653). The **revocation** must also be *communicated* to the offeree:

KEY CASE

Byrne v ***Van Tienhoven*** **(1880) 5 CPD 344**

Concerning: communication of revocation

Facts

On 1 October, a letter offering to sell tinplates was posted from Van Tienhoven in Cardiff to Byrne in New York.

On 8 October, the offerors changed their minds and posted a letter of revocation withdrawing the offer made by letter on 1 October.

On 11 October, Byrne received the letter offering to sell (from 1 October) and accepted by telegram.

On 15 October, Byrne confirmed the acceptance (from 11 October) by letter.

On 20 October, Byrne received the letter of 8 October withdrawing the offer.

Legal principle

The offer of 1 October had not been withdrawn at the time that it was accepted and therefore the contract was formed on acceptance on 11 October. This was so despite the lack of agreement between the parties.

✎ EXAM TIP

Exam questions involving offer and acceptance often involve the communication of revocation between the parties. Remember that an offer is valid until it is revoked and that the revocation must be communicated to the offeree. It is often useful when faced with a question involving facts relating to contract formation to draw a timeline as to 'what happened when' and then to analyse each stage in turn. An example of such a timeline will be provided later in this chapter once we have considered acceptance.

Although any revocation of an offer must be communicated, it does not always have to be communicated by the offeror themselves. Revocation made by a third party is valid provided that:

■ the third party is a reliable source of information; and

■ the third party is one on whom both parties can rely (*Dickinson* v *Dodds* (1876) 2 Ch D 463).

The situation is different with regard to unilateral offers. Since a unilateral offer is a promise in return for an act, it may be accepted by anyone who performs the act stipulated in the offer. Therefore, in order to revoke a unilateral offer (to the world at large) the offeror must take reasonable steps to notify those persons who might be likely to accept. *Shuey* v *United States* (1875) 92 US 73 is the generally accepted authority for this proposition, although it is an American case and therefore carries only persuasive authority in England and Wales.

If the offeree has started performance of the act specified in a unilateral offer then it may not be revoked, even if the act is incomplete.

KEY CASE

Errington v *Errington & Woods* [1952] 1 KB 290

Concerning: revocation of a unilateral offer

Facts

A father bought a house with a mortgage for his son and daughter-in-law to live in. He promised that he would transfer legal title to the property to them if they paid off all the mortgage repayments. The couple did not make any promise in return. The father died after some repayments had been made. Other family members claimed possession of the house, title to which remained in the name of the father. Their claim failed.

Legal principle

The contract was a unilateral contract, since it involved an act (payment of the mortgage) in return for a promise (to transfer the house once all the payments had been made). Once performance had commenced (by the mortgage repayments being made) then the father's promise could not be revoked. However, Lord Denning also stated that the promise would not be binding if the act was left incomplete and unperformed. Therefore, as long as the couple continued to make all the mortgage payments until it was fully paid off then the father's promise to transfer the house to them would still be binding.

The principle from *Errington* v *Errington & Woods* was also accepted by the Court of Appeal *obiter* in the later case of *Daulia Ltd* v *Four Millbank Nominees Ltd* [1978] Ch 231 where Goff LJ stated that:

> In unilateral contracts the offeror is entitled to require full performance of the condition imposed otherwise he is not bound. That must be subject to one important qualification – there must be an implied obligation on the part of the offeror not to prevent the condition being satisfied, an obligation which arises as soon as the offeree starts to perform. Until then the offeror can revoke the whole thing, but once the offeree has embarked on performance, it is too late for the offeror to revoke his offer.

Lapse of time

An offer may not stay open for ever. An offer may state that it is to terminate on a particular date or after a certain fixed period, after which it is no longer capable of acceptance.

Alternatively, where there is no particular date specified for the offer to terminate, then it will in any case lapse after a reasonable time has passed.

KEY CASE

> ### *Ramsgate Victoria Hotel Co Ltd* v *Montefiore* (1866) LR 1 Ex 109
>
> *Concerning: lapse of offer; reasonable time*
>
> **Facts**
>
> The claimant had offered to buy shares in the hotel company in June, but the company did not issue the shares for sale until November.
>
> **Legal principle**
>
> The court held that an offer would lapse after a 'reasonable time'. What is reasonable would depend on the offer and the subject matter of the contract. In cases where the value of the subject matter of the contract could fluctuate rapidly (like the shares in this particular case) or where the subject matter was perishable, then the offer would terminate after a short time.

This principle is also true of offers made by telegram (*Quenerduaine* v *Cole* (1883) 32 WR 185) or similar expedient means of communication such as telex (a system of telegraphy in which printed messages are transmitted and received by teleprinters using the public telecommunication lines) or fax.

Failure to comply with a condition precedent

An offer may also terminate if the parties to it had agreed to meet certain conditions and then failed to do so. For instance, an offer to sell a car on hire-purchase was considered to be subject to the condition that it would remain in the same condition from the time of the offer to the time of acceptance. Therefore, when the car in question had been damaged due to its being stolen from the showroom before the contract was concluded, the offer was rendered incapable of being accepted (*Financings Ltd* v *Stimson* [1962] 1 WLR 1184). The same situation applies where job offers are made subject to satisfactory references, Criminal Records Bureau checks or medical reports.

Death of one of the parties

Death of the offeror

Where the offeror dies before the offer is accepted, then the offeror's personal representatives may still be bound by an acceptance provided that:

- the contract does not involve the personal services of the deceased; and
- the offeree is ignorant of the offeror's death (*Bradbury* v *Morgan* (1862) 1 H & C 249).

Death of the offeree

Where the offeree dies before acceptance, then the offer lapses and the offeree's personal representatives will be unable to accept on behalf of the deceased (*Reynolds* v *Atherton* (1921) 125 LT 690).

■ Acceptance

KEY DEFINITION: Acceptance

An acceptance is a final and unqualified expression of assent to the terms of an offer.

G.H. Treitel, *The Law of Contract* (Sweet & Maxwell, London, 2003) 16

Since **acceptance** is a final and unqualified assent to the terms of an offer, it must correspond exactly with the offer made. It must be unequivocal and unconditional.

KEY DEFINITION: Mirror image rule

The principle that a valid acceptance must correspond exactly with the terms of the offer is sometimes referred to as the mirror image rule.

Counter offers

Since an acceptance must correspond exactly with the terms of the offer in order for it to be valid, it follows that a response that introduces new terms or attempts to vary terms proposed in the offer is not valid. In this case the response becomes a *counter offer* which destroys the original offer, rendering it incapable of acceptance.

KEY CASE

Hyde v *Wrench* (1840) 49 ER 132

Concerning: acceptance; counter offer

Facts

Wrench offered to sell a farm to Hyde for £1,000. Hyde rejected this price and offered to pay £950. Wrench rejected Hyde's offer. Wrench then sold the farm to a third party. Hyde attempted to accept the original offered price of £1,000 and sue Wrench for breach of contract when Wrench sold the farm to another party.

Legal principle

Hyde's claim was rejected. The court held that the counter offer of £950 had impliedly rejected the original offer and, since the original offer had been destroyed, it was no longer open for Hyde to accept.

Lord Langdale stated that:

> If [the offer] had at once been unconditionally accepted, there would undoubtedly have been a perfect binding contract; instead of that, the plaintiff [now referred to as the claimant] made an offer of his own, to purchase the property for £950, and he thereby rejected the offer previously made by the defendant. I think that it was not afterwards competent for him to revive the proposal of the defendant, by tendering an acceptance of it; and that, therefore, there exists no obligation of any sort between the parties.

Since a counter offer destroys the original offer, the roles of offeror and offeree become reversed. The party who made the original offer may accept the counter offer, reject the counter offer, or make a counter offer in return (in which case the roles reverse again). This can continue until agreement is finally reached as depicted in Figure 1.3.

Figure 1.3

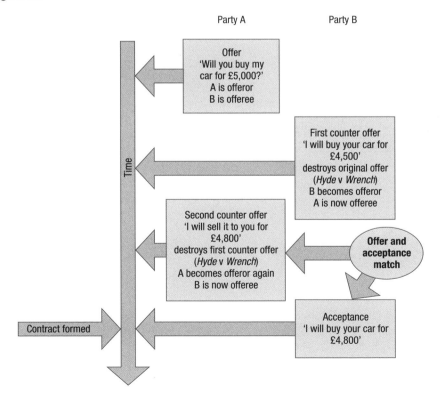

Requests for information

A mere request for information is treated differently to a counter offer.

KEY CASE

Stevenson, Jacques & Co v *McLean* (1880) 5 QBD 346

Concerning: acceptance; request for information

Facts

McLean telegraphed Stevenson offering to sell 3,800 tons of iron 'at 40 s net cash per ton, open till Monday'. On Monday morning Stevenson telegrammed McLean: 'Please wire whether you would accept forty for delivery over two months or if not longest limit you would give.' McLean did not respond and at 1.34 p.m. Stevenson telegrammed again, accepting the original offer. McLean had already sold the iron to a third party of which he advised Stevenson by telegram at 1.25 p.m. That telegram crossed with Stevenson's second telegram. Stevenson sued for breach of contract.

Legal principle

Stevenson's first telegram was not a counter offer. It was a mere request for information. Consequently, McLean's offer was still open at 1.34 p.m. It was validly accepted. Therefore, there was a valid contract of which McLean was in breach. As Lush J said:

> Here there is no counter-proposal. The words are: 'Please wire whether you would accept forty for delivery over two months, or if not, the longest limit you would give.' There is nothing specific by way of offer or rejection, but a mere inquiry, which should have been answered and not treated as a rejection of the offer.

Therefore, if a response is made to an offer that does not attempt to vary the terms of the offer it is not a counter offer, since it does not reject the terms of the offer. It is therefore still open to acceptance by the offeree.

✎ **EXAM TIP**

Once you have identified an offer in the facts of a problem question, look out for any communications from the offeree and analyse these to determine whether they amount to a request for information (which allows the original offer to stand) or whether they amount to a counter offer (which destroys the original offer and takes its place). A key distinction here is whether the offeree is asking for more detail (request for information) or whether he is suggesting an alternative set of terms (a counter offer).

Standard form contracts

Problems can arise where one or both parties uses pre-prepared contract forms in relation to the general rule that the acceptance must correspond exactly to the offer.

KEY DEFINITION: Battle of the forms

The situation that arises where one or both of the parties attempt to rely on their standard terms is often referred to as the battle of the forms.

This situation may arise as follows:

- A makes an offer to B on a form containing A's standard terms of business.
- B 'accepts' A's offer on a form containing B's standard terms of business.
- A's standard terms and B's standard terms conflict.

At this stage, there is no contract, since offer and acceptance do not match. Generally speaking, in the case of conflict, each communication is considered to be a counter offer so that if a contract is formed (in such cases acceptance is usually inferred by conduct – see later in this chapter) then it must be on the terms of the last counter offer. This is deemed to have been accepted and it is the terms of the final counter offer which apply to the contract as a whole (see for example *Zambia Steel & Building Supplies Ltd* v *James Clark & Eaton Ltd* [1986] 2 Lloyd's Rep 225).

In *British Road Services* v *Arthur V. Crutchley Ltd* [1968] 1 WLR 811 the claimants had delivered a quantity of whisky to the defendants for storage. The delivery driver handed the defendants a delivery note which incorporated the claimants' 'conditions of carriage'. This note was stamped by the defendants as 'Received under [the defendants'] conditions'. This was held to be a counter offer which the claimants had accepted by handing over the goods and therefore the contract incorporated the defendants' and not the claimants' conditions.

Although the courts may decide that there is no valid agreement and halt performance of the contract, they are reluctant to do so once performance has started (*British Steel Corporation* v *Cleveland Bridge and Engineering Co* [1984] 1 All ER 504).

However, a somewhat radical (and thus unlikely to be followed) departure from the strict offer/counter-offer analysis was offered in *Butler Machine Tool Co Ltd* v *Ex-Cell-O Corporation (England) Ltd* [1979] 1 WLR 401 by Lord Denning, who looked beyond the strict wording of the forms when he stated (at 404H) that:

> In most cases when there is a 'battle of the forms', there is a contract as soon as the last of the forms is sent and received without objection being taken to it . . . the difficulty is to decide which form, or which part of which form, is a term or condition of the contract.

In some cases, the battle is won by the man who fires the last shot. He is the man who puts forward the latest terms and conditions: and if they are not objected to by the other party, he may be taken to have agreed to them . . . There are yet some cases where the battle depends on the shots fired on both sides. There is a concluded contract but the forms vary. If . . . they are mutually contradictory . . . then the conflicting terms may have to be scrapped and replaced by a reasonable implication.

A more recent '**battle of the forms**' case can be found in *GHSP Inc* v *AB Electronic Ltd* [2010] EWHC 1828 (Comm). Here, the court was satisfied that the contract was not concluded on either party's terms and conditions due to the lack of consensus and the parties had already agreed that the implied terms as set out in the Sale of Goods Act 1979 would apply if neither party's terms were found to apply. Therefore, when there is a 'battle of the forms' the court may find that a contract was not concluded on either party's terms and rely on statutory implied terms instead. However, if it is clear that there is such disagreement between the parties that any contract concluded would not be on either set of terms, it is likely that Lord Denning's 'last shot' rule will continue to apply.

In *Transformers & Rectifiers Ltd* v *Needs Ltd* [2015] EWHC 269 (TCC) the court held that **neither** side had sufficiently introduced their standard terms for the terms to be included in a contract.

Tenders

Since an invitation to tender is usually an invitation to treat, the submission of a tender is usually an offer. However, the 'acceptance' of a tender does not always result in a binding contract:

■ Where the tender is submitted for supplying specific goods or services on a specific date, acceptance results in a binding contract.

■ Where the tender is submitted for supplying a specific quantity of goods over a specified period of time, acceptance results in a binding contract.

■ Where the tender is submitted for indefinite subject matter such as 'such quantities as you may order' or 'as and when required' then 'acceptance' of that tender does not result in a binding contract at that time. Acceptance occurs when an order is placed (*Percival* v *London County Council Asylum, etc Committee* (1918) 87 LJ KB 677). Once an order is placed, the party who submitted the tender (the offer) is bound (*Great Northern Railway* v *Witham* (1873) LR 9 CP 16).

Communication of acceptance

Generally speaking, an acceptance has no effect until it is communicated to the offeror. In *Entores* v *Miles Far East Corporation* [1955] 2 QB 327 Lord Denning explained the principle as follows:

Let me first consider a case where two people make a contract by word of mouth in the presence of one another. Suppose, for instance, that I shout an offer to a man across a river or a courtyard but I do not hear his reply because it is drowned by an aircraft flying overhead. There is no contract at that moment. If he wishes to make a contract, he must wait till the aircraft is gone and then shout back his acceptance so that I can hear what he says. Not until I have his answer am I bound.

Silence cannot amount to acceptance

Since acceptance must be communicated, it follows that silence can never constitute acceptance.

KEY CASE

Felthouse v *Bindley* (1863) 142 ER 1037

Concerning: acceptance; silence

Facts

An uncle and nephew were negotiating the sale of the nephew's horse. The uncle had stated that 'if I hear no more from you I shall consider the horse mine at £30 15/-'.

The nephew did not reply but asked an auctioneer to withdraw the horse from an auction. The auctioneer forgot the instruction and the horse was sold to another party. In order to claim against the auctioneer, the uncle needed to prove that there was a contract between him and his nephew for the sale of the horse.

Legal principle

The court held that there was no contract since the nephew had never communicated his intention to accept to his uncle 'or done anything to bind himself'.

This principle was also considered in *The Leonidas D* [1985] 1 WLR 925 where Goff LJ commented that it was 'axiomatic that acceptance of an offer cannot be inferred from silence, save in the most exceptional circumstances'.

Acceptance in unilateral contracts

In a **unilateral contract**, the rule that acceptance must be communicated is waived:

- The offer can be accepted by fully performing the stipulated act or forbearance (*Daulia Ltd* v *Four Millbank Nominees Ltd*).
- There is no need to communicate acceptance to the offeror (*Carlill* v *Carbolic Smoke Ball Company*; *Bowerman* v *Association of British Travel Agents* [1995] NLJ 1815).
- The offer can be withdrawn before it is accepted: the offer being accepted only by *some* performance.

✎ EXAM TIP

If you are dealing with a unilateral offer in a problem question, determine whether it has been accepted by asking yourself the following questions:

- What conduct did the offeror specify was required?
- What did the offeree do and did this match what the offeror required?
- If the offeree has done only part of what the offeror wanted, did the offeror intervene to prevent the offeree completing performance?
- Did the offeror have a change of heart and withdraw the offer? Did this happen before or after the offeree had embarked on performance?

Acceptance by conduct

Acceptance may be inferred from conduct without it being expressly communicated.

KEY CASE

Brogden v *Metropolitan Railway Co* (1877) 2 App Cas 666

Concerning: acceptance by conduct

Facts

Brogden was a colliery owner in Wales who supplied the Metropolitan Railway Company. In November 1871 a representative of Brogden suggested that a contract should be entered into. A draft contract was prepared and sent to Brogden, who filled in the arbitration clause by nominating an arbitrator, appended the word 'Approved' and returned it to the railway. The railway's agent did not acknowledge it. In December 1871 the railway placed an order on the terms of the document, which Brogden fulfilled. The parties traded on the terms of the document until December 1873, when Brogden refused to continue to supply on that basis. The railway brought an action against Brogden for breach of contract. Brogden claimed that since the railway had never acknowledged the altered draft, which was a counter offer, there was no contract.

Legal principle

The House of Lords accepted that the completion of the arbitrator's name technically rendered it a counter offer. However, since the parties to the contract had traded on the terms of the contract then they had accepted the counter offer as part of the agreement and Brogden, therefore, could not claim that there was no contract.

Stipulated methods of acceptance

Although acceptance can generally be in any form, as long as it is communicated to the offeree (other than in the case of a unilateral contract), where the offer stipulates a particular method of acceptance, such as 'by return of post', 'by fax' or 'by telegram', then if the offeree uses a different method there may not be a contract (*Eliason* v *Henshaw* (1819) 4 Wheaton 225; 4 US (L Ed) 556) if the offeror clearly states that *only the stipulated method of acceptance will be sufficient.*

If the offeree uses an equally expeditious method of acceptance to that stipulated, then that should be sufficient. In *Tinn* v *Hoffmann* (1873) 29 LT 271 the offeree was instructed to reply to an offer 'by return of post' to which Honeyman J said: 'That does not mean exclusively a reply by letter or return of post, but you may reply by telegram or by verbal message or by any other means not later than a letter written by return of post.' This principle was also applied in *Manchester Diocesan Council for Education* v *Commercial & General Investments Ltd* [1970] 1 WLR 241 such that an acceptance which meets the offeror's objective in prescribing a method of acceptance (albeit not by the method prescribed) will remain valid.

Finally, if the offer does not state a method of acceptance, the required speed of acceptance can be deduced from the means by which the offer was sent: therefore, for example, if an offer is made by telegram, then it is implied that acceptance should be made by an equally speedy means. Therefore, an acceptance by post would be ineffective (*Quenerduaine* v *Cole*).

Acceptance by post – the postal rule

Acceptance by post is an exception to the general rule that acceptance must come to the attention of the offeror before it is valid.

KEY CASE

Adams v *Lindsell* (1818) 1 B & Ald 681

Concerning: acceptance by post; the 'postal rule'

Facts

Lindsell made an offer by post to sell Adams some wool, asking for a reply 'in course of post'. The offer letter was sent on 2 September, but it did not arrive until 5 September, whereupon Adams posted a letter of acceptance at once. By the time the letter of acceptance had arrived (which was after some lengthy time), Lindsell, who had assumed that his offer had been rejected, had sold the wool to a third party. Adams claimed breach of contract.

Legal principle

The court held that the contract was made at the time the letter was posted.

❗ Don't be tempted to . . .

You must remember that the postal rule (if it applies at all) *applies to acceptances only, and not to the revocation of an offer by post.* It is a very common error to state that an offer was revoked by letter at the time that the letter was posted because of the postal rule. Be careful to avoid falling into this trap.

Therefore, the general 'postal rule' is that acceptance by post takes effect upon posting rather than delivery. However, there are certain conditions that relate to its use.

For the postal rule to apply:

- Acceptance by post must have been requested by the offeror, or acceptance by post must be a normal, reasonable or anticipated means of acceptance (*Henthorn* v *Fraser* [1892] 2 Ch 27).

- The letter of acceptance must be properly stamped and addressed (*Re London & Northern Bank, ex parte Jones* [1990] 1 Ch 220).

- The letter of acceptance must be posted – that is, in the control of the Post Office (or whatever the universal postal service is called from time to time: *Brinkibon* v *Stahag Stahl* [1983] 2 AC 34). In *Re London & Northern Bank, ex parte Jones* a letter of acceptance that had been handed to a postman who was authorised only to *deliver* (not collect) was held *not* to have been posted.

- The postal rule must not have been expressly excluded in the offer. In *Holwell Securities* v *Hughes* [1974] 1 WLR 155 it was held that an offer which required acceptance 'by notice in writing' meant that actual communication of acceptance must reach the offeror and as such the claimants could not rely on the postal rule to assert the existence of a contract.

- Use of the postal rule must not create 'manifest inconvenience or absurdity' (*Holwell Securities* v *Hughes*).

✎ EXAM TIP

The postal rule is often encountered in problem questions on contract formation. Although most students conclude that where a letter of acceptance has been posted then the postal rule applies, the vast majority of those often forget to discuss the conditions which apply to the postal rule. However, you should see from this section that there are several provisos to the use of the postal rule. You can improve your answer by a brief consideration of the conditions which apply to the postal rule. While these exceptions may not apply to your particular question, in considering them, and supporting those considerations with case authority, you will have demonstrated a far greater depth of understanding which should make your answer stand out.

The postal rule also applies:

- if the letter of acceptance is received after notice of revocation of the offer has been sent (*Henthorn* v *Fraser*);
- if the letter of acceptance is *never* received by the offeror (*Household Fire Insurance Co* v *Grant* (1879) 4 Ex D 216).

Non-instantaneous communication of acceptance

Since the postal rule was developed, advances in communications technology have led to a number of situations where its use is irrelevant. Virtually instantaneous communications methods, such as telephone conversations, are treated in the same way as face-to-face personal conversations and are, therefore, relatively unproblematic: acceptance takes place when and where the acceptance is received (*Entores* v *Miles Far East Corporation*).

However, the situation is more difficult when answering machines are used. A message may be left which is not played back for some time. The same is true of telex, fax and email: all systems (when working correctly) deliver messages virtually instantaneously, but those messages may not be read instantly if the receiving party is away from the receiving machine. The question then becomes one of if, when and where a contract is formed with such non-instantaneous methods.

KEY CASE

Brinkibon v *Stahag Stahl* [1983] 2 AC 34

Concerning: acceptance by non-instantaneous communications

Facts

An acceptance was sent by telex out of office hours.

Legal principle

The House of Lords held that a telex message that was sent outside office hours should not be considered to be an instantaneous means of communication and therefore acceptance could be effective only when the office re-opened.

Lord Wilberforce summarised the situation in relation to modern communications methods by stating that:

No universal rule can cover all such cases; they must be resolved by reference to the intention of the parties, by sound business practice and in some cases by a judgment where the risk should lie.

Communications within office hours to machines are generally considered to be actual communications since the person sending the message has done all that they could reasonably be expected to do to bring the communication to the attention of the recipient (*Tenax Steamship Co Ltd* v *The Brimnes (Owners) (The Brimnes)* [1975] QB 929). Outside office hours, it is expected that the communication will be read on the next working day (*Mondial Shipping and Chartering BV* v *Astarte Shipping Ltd* [1995] CLC 1011). In *Thomas* v *BPE Solicitors* [2010] EWHC 206 (Ch), Blair J considered *obiter* that the 'office hours receipt' rule applies to acceptances by email (although he did not consider 6 p.m. to be outside working hours, even though the intended recipient had in fact gone home 15 minutes earlier).

A good example of difficulties that can arise where there are several emails in a chain of correspondence and which involves the application of the principles concerning revocation of offers and counter offers can be found in *Grant* v *Bragg* [2009] EWCA Civ 1228; [2010] 1 All ER (Comm) 1166, *on appeal from* [2009] EWHC 74 (Ch); [2009] 1 All ER (Comm) 674).

■ Intention to create legal relations

In order to prevent the courts from being troubled by disputes concerning agreements which are not intended to be legally binding, the courts have sought to distinguish agreements that should be legally enforceable and those which should not.

These fall into a number of categories:

- social and domestic agreements
- commercial agreements
- advertisements.

Social and domestic agreements

There is a presumption that there is no intention to create legal relations in social or domestic agreements. This presumption may be rebutted.

Husbands and wives

Agreements between husband and wife are presumed not to create legal relations unless the agreement itself states that it does.

KEY CASE

***Balfour* v *Balfour* [1919] 2 KB 571**

Concerning: intention to create legal relations

Facts

A husband worked overseas and his wife lived with him overseas. They came back to England during his leave. The wife developed rheumatoid arthritis and her doctor advised her not to return overseas. The husband promised to pay £30 per month until she was able to return overseas. The husband eventually wrote to say that it was better that they remained separated. The wife sued to enforce continued payment of the £30 monthly.

Legal principle

The Court of Appeal held that the agreement was not enforceable since there was a general presumption that there is no intention to create legal relations between family members.

In *Balfour,* the couple were not separated at the time of making their agreement. The Court of Appeal stated that the principle from *Balfour* did not apply where the couple were not living together amicably, about to separate or, indeed, had separated. In these cases, the parties are considered to be required to sort out their finances in more precise terms and therefore any agreement between them is more likely to carry an intention to create legal relations (and hence to be legally binding) (*Merritt* v *Merritt* [1970] 1 WLR 1211).

Parents and children

Domestic agreements between parents and children are presumed not to create legal relations (*Jones* v *Padavatton* [1969] 1 WLR 328).

Parties sharing a house

Where an agreement is made between parties who share a dwelling but are not related, then the court will consider all the circumstances of the agreement. They are more likely to find the intention to be legally bound where money has changed hands (*Simpkins* v *Pays* [1955] 1 WLR 975).

Other social agreements

The courts are reluctant to find contractual intention in social agreements. For instance, in *Lens* v *Devonshire Club* (1914) *The Times,* 4 December, it was held that the winner of a competition held by a golf club could not sue for his prize since 'no one concerned with that competition ever intended that there should be any legal results flowing from the conditions posted and the acceptance by the competitor of those conditions'.

Commercial agreements

Just as there is a presumption that there is no intention to create legal relations in social or domestic agreements the converse is true in commercial agreements: it is presumed that there is an intention to create legal relations.

This presumption can generally be rebutted only by express provision in the contract. In *Rose & Frank Co* v *Crompton Bros Ltd* [1925] AC 445 it was held that a commercial agreement between a British manufacturer and their appointed distributor in the USA which expressly stated that it was 'not subject to legal jurisdiction' in either country was sufficient to rebut the presumption that it was intended to be a contract.

This is so even if the agreement appears to be gratuitous in nature, such as those involving an *ex gratia* payment (*Edwards* v *Skyways* [1969] 1 WLR 349).

However, it does not apply to so-called 'comfort letters' which are interpreted as a statement of fact rather than as a contractual promise (*Kleinwort Benson Ltd* v *Malaysian Mining Corporation* [1989] 1 WLR 379). It also does not apply to agreements (such as the football pools) which are stated to be 'binding in honour only' (*Jones* v *Vernons Pools* [1938] 2 All ER 626).

Advertisements

Sellers often make claims in advertisements that are generally treated as a 'mere puff' and as such do not generally create legal relations. However, more specific pledges, such as 'we are never knowingly undersold, so if we find a competitor within the area selling the same product that is part of our own standard offer at a lower price, our shelf price will be reduced to match', are likely to be binding. A statement will not be binding if the court considers that it was not seriously meant (*Weeks* v *Tybald* (1605) Noy 11).

■ Putting it all together

Answer guidelines

See the sample question at the start of the chapter.

Approaching the question

This question is concerned with contract formation. Chris's legal position will depend on the exact timing of communication of revocation and acceptance. The best place to approach a question like this, which involves complex timing issues, is to start untangling the facts. You can do this by constructing a timeline as shown in Figure 1.4. Once you have your timeline, you can then begin to analyse each event in turn in terms of offer, acceptance and revocation.

Figure 1.4

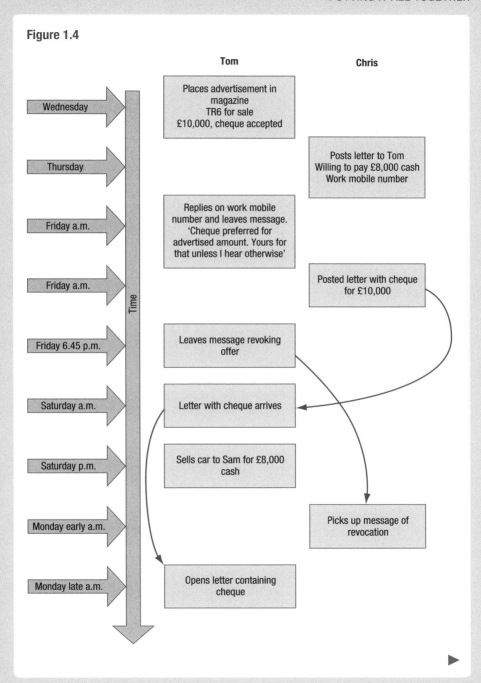

Important points to include

- The advertisement is likely to be construed as an *invitation to treat* (*Partridge* v *Crittenden*) – that is an expression of willingness to accept offers – rather than as a unilateral offer (*Carlill*).

- Therefore, since an invitation to treat can only be followed by an offer, Chris's letter on Thursday is an *offer* to buy the car for £8,000 in cash.

- This offer is effective upon receipt by Tom on Friday morning. The postal rule does not apply to offers, only acceptances (*Adams* v *Lindsell*).

- Tom's voicemail message in return on Friday morning in which he states he will sell only for the 'advertised amount' and would prefer payment by cheque does not match the offer made by Chris. It is therefore a counter offer that destroys Chris's offer (*Hyde* v *Wrench*).

- Tom's statement of 'yours for that unless I hear from you to the contrary' has no effect since silence cannot constitute acceptance (*Felthouse* v *Bindley*).

- Upon listening to the voicemail, Chris sends an acceptance with a cheque for £10,000 by post. This acceptance matches the terms of the offer precisely (cheque, £10,000).

- Does the postal rule apply? (*Adams* v *Lindsell*). If so, it does not matter that the acceptance letter was not opened until late Monday morning; indeed, it would not matter if the letter never arrived (*Household Fire Insurance Co* v *Grant*). It would be effective on posting and the contract would have been formed at that point on Friday morning.

- There is nothing to suggest that the letter was improperly addressed or posted and Tom did not specify any specific means of acceptance (*Holwell Securities* v *Hughes*).

- Tom could argue that the postal rule does not apply since a letter is not an appropriate means of response to a voicemail message (*Quenerduaine* v *Cole*; *Henthorn* v *Fraser*).

- On Friday evening Tom left a further voicemail message of revocation. Since this was outside normal office hours, the message is deemed not to have been communicated at this time. In general, instantaneous communications take place when and where received and the postal rule does not apply (*Entores* v *Miles Far East Corporation*). However, following *Brinkibon* v *Stahag Stahl*, no universal rule exists and the courts can take into account the intention of the parties, sound business practices and an assessment of where the risk should lie. Tom's voicemail message of revocation is therefore likely to be deemed as communicated on Monday morning when Chris's office re-opens for business and Chris accesses the messages on his work mobile.

- If the postal rule applies then Chris will have a contract for the car. Tom will also have a contract with Sam for the car. Tom will be in breach of one of these contracts.

- Remedies that may be available to Chris will be discussed further in Chapter 9.

Make your answer stand out

- Although the question is concerned primarily with offer and acceptance, remember that these are only two of the essential elements of a contract. Although intention to create legal relations and consideration are unproblematic in this instance, a thorough answer will consider them both briefly. Since this is a commercial arrangement (Tom is a vintage car dealer) then the presumption that there is intention to create legal relations arises (there is nothing to suggest that it has been rebutted: *Rose & Frank Co* v *Crompton Bros Ltd*). Consideration will be satisfied by the price paid for the car (see Chapter 2).

- In a question like this it is important to adopt a methodical approach to avoid a confused or rambling answer that is difficult for the marker to follow. If you are not expressing your line of argument with sufficient clarity you will lose marks. A structured method that breaks each stage of the transaction down in time and deals with each in turn may help in this respect. Remember your problem-solving technique – set out the legal issue that needs to be resolved and the law that applies to it before going on to apply the law to the particular facts of the case and reaching a conclusion on each particular issue. You may remember this legal problem approach by the mnemonic IRAC (Issue – Rule – Application – Conclusion).

READ TO IMPRESS

Austen-Baker, R. (2006) Offeree silence and contractual agreement. *Common Law World Review*, 35(4): 247.

McKendrick, E. (1991) Invitations to tender and the creation of contracts. *Lloyd's Maritime and Commercial Law Quarterly*, 31.

Mitchell, P. and Phillips, J. (2002) The contractual nexus: is reliance essential? *Oxford Journal of Legal Studies*, 22: 115.

Steyn, J. (1997) Contract law: fulfilling the reasonable expectations of honest men. *Law Quarterly Review*, 113: 433.

www.pearsoned.co.uk/lawexpress

 Go online to access more revision support including quizzes to test your knowledge, sample questions with answer guidelines, podcasts you can download, and more!

Consideration and promissory estoppel

2

Revision checklist

Essential points you should know:

- [ ] The definition of consideration
- [ ] The rules relating to 'good' consideration
- [ ] The exceptions to the general rule that performance of an existing duty is not good consideration
- [ ] The rules relating to part payment of debts
- [ ] The development and operation of promissory estoppel

■ Topic map

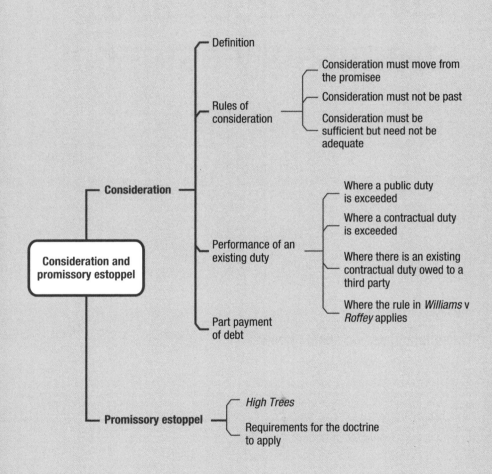

Definition

Rules of consideration
- Consideration must move from the promisee
- Consideration must not be past
- Consideration must be sufficient but need not be adequate

Consideration

Performance of an existing duty
- Where a public duty is exceeded
- Where a contractual duty is exceeded
- Where there is an existing contractual duty owed to a third party
- Where the rule in *Williams* v *Roffey* applies

Part payment of debt

Consideration and promissory estoppel

Promissory estoppel
- *High Trees*
- Requirements for the doctrine to apply

A printable version of this topic map is available from **www.pearsoned.co.uk/lawexpress**

■ Introduction

Consideration is generally one of the essential elements of a binding contract.

Therefore, when offer, acceptance, intention to create legal relations (Chapter 1) and consideration are present, an agreement becomes contractually binding. This chapter will review what is meant by consideration and consolidate your revision of the various rules that have developed around it. It will also look at the doctrine of promissory estoppel, which is a notable exception to the general rule that promises are binding only if supported by consideration.

ASSESSMENT ADVICE

Essay questions

Essay questions on consideration are relatively common. Since consideration is a topic that sets out a few basic principles, each of which has a number of exceptions, rules or modifications, then it is quite easy to set an essay that requires you to consider one or more areas within the topic and explore its rules of operation in depth. As with any essay question, it is important to have a good in-depth knowledge of the area and its supporting cases. This will enable you to demonstrate your knowledge in applying the subject matter directly to the question at hand.

Problem questions

Problem questions may also involve consideration. Even in a contract formation question, such as that in Chapter 1, consideration should be discussed briefly, even if it is uncontentious or unproblematic – where it is usually satisfied by the price paid in exchange for goods or services. However, you may encounter a more specific question on consideration that raises issues surrounding its timing, its adequacy or sufficiency or how it applies in cases where there is an existing contractual duty or the part payment of a debt. For these questions it is important to equip yourself with the knowledge of the rules of consideration as they apply to a particular area.

■ Sample question

Could you answer this question? Below is a typical essay question that could arise on this topic. Guidelines on answering the question are included at the end of the chapter, while a sample problem question and guidance on tackling it can be found on the companion website.

ESSAY QUESTION

To what extent does the doctrine of promissory estoppel prevent a party to a contract from enforcing their legal rights?

◼ Consideration

Generally speaking, a promise is not contractually binding unless it is either made in a deed or supported by some **consideration**. English law will not enforce a gratuitous (that is, done without charge, payment or any value given in return) promise – therefore, if I promise to clean your windows, you may force me to do so only if you have provided some consideration in return. This may be in the form of payment ('I promise to give you £10 in return for your promise to clean my windows') or some other service ('I promise to fix your washing machine in return for your promise to clean my windows'). In other words, a person to whom a promise is made (the promisee) has to give some consideration in order to render the otherwise gratuitous promise made in their favour into a legally binding contractual agreement.

Definition

The definition of consideration arises from case law.

KEY CASE

Currie v *Misa* (1875) LR 10 Ex 153

Concerning: consideration; definition

Facts

This case involved a dispute concerning the stopped payment of a cheque; however the facts are not important to the legal principle stated below.

Legal principle

Lush J referred to consideration as follows:

> A valuable consideration, in the sense of the law, may consist either of some right, interest, profit or benefit accruing to the one party, or some forbearance, detriment, loss or responsibility, given, suffered or undertaken by the other.

A more sophisticated definition was provided in 1876 by Pollock in *Principles of Contract* which was approved by the House of Lords.

KEY CASE

Dunlop v *Selfridge* [1915] AC 847

Concerning: consideration; definition

Facts

The facts of this case are given in Chapter 3 since they are relevant to the doctrine of privity of contract. The case also provided a definition of consideration which is set out in the legal principle below.

Legal principle

Lord Dunedin approved Pollock's definition of consideration:

> An act of forbearance or the promise thereof is the price for which the promise of the other is bought, and the promise thus given for value is enforceable.

Rules of consideration

There are a number of rules surrounding the operation of consideration that have built up from case law. In summary:

- consideration must move from the promisee;
- consideration must not be past;
- consideration must be sufficient but need not be adequate.

Consideration must move from the promisee

The rule that 'consideration must move from the promisee' means that a person to whom a promise was made can enforce that promise only if they have themselves provided the consideration for it. The promise cannot be enforced if the consideration moved from a third party.

KEY CASE

Tweddle v *Atkinson* (1861) 121 ER 762

Concerning: consideration must move from the promisee   ▶

Facts

William, the son of John Tweddle, and the daughter of William Guy intended to marry. John Tweddle agreed with William Guy in writing that both should pay money to the husband, William Tweddle. William Guy died before paying money to William Tweddle. Guy's executors refused to pay the money to Tweddle. He sued the executors to the estate.

Legal principle

William Tweddle's claim failed. Even though he was named in the agreement, he had not himself given consideration for the agreement.

This situation can be depicted as shown in Figure 2.1.

Figure 2.1

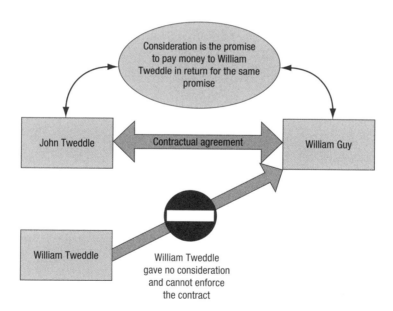

William Tweddle was also unable to enforce the contract due to the common law rule on privity of contract. This is covered in Chapter 3. You must remember that this sort of agreement may now be subject to the Contracts (Rights of Third Parties) Act 1999, which is also considered in Chapter 3.

Consideration must not be past

To understand what this means, it is necessary to explain three different types of consideration:

- executory consideration
- executed consideration
- past consideration.

Executory consideration

Executory consideration arises where promises are exchanged to perform acts in the future: for example, if I promise to deliver you an extra-large pizza and you promise to pay on delivery. This is a bilateral contract (a promise in exchange for a promise) and is enforceable: therefore, if I deliver your extra-large pizza and you do not pay, then I can sue you for breach of contract.

Executed consideration

Executed consideration arises where one party performs an act in order to fulfil a promise made by the other. This situation is typical of 'reward' contracts: if I offer £100 to anyone who can provide information that helps me track down my long-lost sister and you do so, then I am bound to pay you under this unilateral contract.

Past consideration

The basic principle is that the consideration for a promise must be given in return for that promise. Therefore, if I clean your windows and, once I am done, you promise to pay me £10 for doing so, then I cannot enforce your promise since I did not clean your windows in return for that promise – the promise was made *after* the act was done.

Re McArdle [1951] Ch 669

Concerning: past consideration

Facts

A son and his wife lived in his mother's house. On her death, the house was to pass to the son and three other children. The son's wife paid for both repairs and improvements ▶

to the property. The mother then made her four children sign an agreement to pay her daughter-in-law back from the proceeds of her estate. The mother died and the children refused to pay.

Legal principle

The daughter-in-law's claim was unsuccessful. She had already performed the act before the promise to pay had been made. Therefore, her consideration was past and the promise to pay was unenforceable.

It follows from this that if a guarantee is made in respect of something after it has been sold then there is no consideration for that guarantee and it is not binding (*Roscorla* v *Thomas* (1842) 3 QB 234).

There is an exception to the general rule that consideration must not be past:

KEY CASE

Lampleigh v Braithwaite (1615) 80 ER 255

Concerning: past consideration; exception to the general rule

Facts

Braithwaite had killed another man and asked Lampleigh to secure a pardon. Lampleigh went to considerable effort and expense to secure the pardon for Braithwaite who subsequently promised to pay Lampleigh £100. Braithwaite then failed to pay the £100. Lampleigh sued.

Legal principle

Lampleigh's claim was successful, even though, on the basis of past consideration, his efforts were in the past in relation to the promise to pay. The court, however, considered that the original request by Braithwaite in fact contained an implied promise that he would reward and reimburse Lampleigh for his efforts: therefore, the previous request and the subsequent promise were part of the same transaction and were enforceable.

Therefore, if services are rendered on request and where both parties understand that payment will be made, the promise may be enforceable even though the consideration is past. The principle was affirmed in *Re Casey's Patents* [1892] 1 Ch 104 with the criteria being restated by Lord Scarman in *Pao On* v *Lau Yiu Long* [1980] AC 614 as follows:

■ The act must have been done at the promisor's request.

- The parties must have understood that the act was to be remunerated further by a payment or the conferment of some other benefit and payment (in other words, an implied promise to pay to be quantified at a later date).
- The payment, or the conferment of a benefit, must have been legally enforceable had it been promised in advance.

Consideration must be sufficient but need not be adequate

As long as the consideration has some value (sufficient to render the promise enforceable) the courts will not concern themselves with its adequacy (whether it represents a good bargain). For instance, if I freely decide to offer to sell you my brand new camera for 20p and you accept, then this is sufficient to render the contract binding even though it is seemingly not a fair exchange.

KEY CASE

Thomas v *Thomas* **(1842) 2 QB 851**

Concerning: sufficiency and adequacy of consideration

Facts

A husband expressed a wish that his wife should be allowed to remain in their house after his death. This was not written in his will. After his death, his executors allowed his wife to stay at a rent of £1 per year. They later tried to dispossess her.

Legal principle

The payment of the 'peppercorn' rent was sufficient consideration for the contract to be enforceable. The husband's wish alone, however, would not have been sufficient consideration for the contract to be enforceable.

In order to be sufficient in law, consideration must be:

- real
- tangible
- valuable (that is, it must have some actual value).

 Make your answer stand out

If you are discussing the idea of consideration it is important to remember that although consideration is straightforward when the value is pecuniary, i.e. can be expressed in terms of a sum of money, this is not the only way in which something can be viewed ▶

as valuable. For example, in *White* v *Bluett* (1853) LJ Ex 36 a son attempted to claim that he did not owe his late father's estate repayment of a sum of money due on a promissory note since he had agreed with his father that the debt would be written off in return for his promise not to complain about his father's will. This promise not to complain was held to be insufficiently tangible to amount to good consideration. However, in *Ward* v *Byham* [1956] 1 WLR 496 a mother's promise to keep her illegitimate child 'well looked after and happy' in return for money towards the child's upkeep from its father was held to be sufficient consideration (since there is no legal duty to keep a child happy). In some instances, apparently worthless items have been held to be good consideration.

KEY CASE

Chappell & Co Ltd v *Nestlé Co Ltd* **[1960] AC 87**

Concerning: sufficiency and adequacy of consideration

Facts

Nestlé were offering a record (the copyright of which was owned by Chappell) for sale at 1s. 6d **plus** three wrappers from their chocolate bars. The record normally sold at 6s. 8d. Permission to use the copyright was not obtained. Chappell sued to prevent the promotion since they would receive a much lower royalty from it.

Legal principle

The wrappers were held to be part of the consideration, even though they were thrown away when received. As Lord Somervell commented:

> It is said that, when received, the wrappers are of no value to Nestlé. This is irrelevant. A contracting party can stipulate for what consideration he chooses. A peppercorn does not cease to be good consideration if it is established that the promisee does not like pepper and will throw away the corn.

Performance of an existing duty

In general, if a party is performing a duty which he is already bound to do then this is not sufficient to amount to consideration for a new agreement. In essence, since consideration is defined in terms of a detriment or forbearance, then it seems logical that you cannot suffer any detriment in relation to a new promise if that detriment is something that you were going to have to do anyway.

This applies to public as well as contractual duties:

KEY CASE

Collins v *Godefroy* (1831) 109 ER 1040

Concerning: consideration; performance of an existing public duty

Facts

A police officer was promised a sum of money by the defendant in a trial in return for the officer giving evidence, since it was important to the defendant that the officer did so. The officer had already been subpoenaed to do so.

Legal principle

The promise to pay was unenforceable since there was no consideration given by the police officer for it. He was already under a legal duty to attend court.

KEY CASE

Stilk v *Myrick* (1809) 170 ER 1168

Concerning: consideration; performance of an existing contractual duty

Facts

A team of eleven sailors agreed to crew a ship from London to the Baltic and back. Two sailors deserted in the Baltic. The remaining nine refused to work, and pressed the captain for higher wages. He agreed at the time but ultimately refused to pay. The sailors sued the captain.

Legal principle

The promise to pay was unenforceable since the sailors were already contractually bound to return the ship to London. Therefore, there was no consideration given by the sailors in return for the captain's promise to pay additional wages.

Therefore, the basic rule in relation to performance of an existing duty is that it is not good consideration for a new promise.

However, there are exceptions to this basic rule:

- where a public duty is exceeded
- where a contractual duty is exceeded
- where there is an existing contractual duty owed to a third party
- where the rule in *Williams* v *Roffey* applies.

Where a public duty is exceeded

KEY CASE

***Glassbrook Bros* v *Glamorgan County Council* [1925] AC 270**

Concerning: consideration; exceeding an existing public duty

Facts

During a miners' strike, the owner of a pit asked the police for extra protection and promised to pay for it. After the strike, the pit owner refused to pay, claiming that the police were already bound by a public duty to protect the pit.

Legal principle

The promise to pay was enforceable: since the police had done more than they would ordinarily have done (in sending additional officers), this was good consideration for the pit owner's promise to pay.

Therefore, if one party ends up giving more than they would otherwise have done, then this *additional* detriment represents sufficient consideration to render a promise given in return for it enforceable. The same principle also applies to contractual duties.

Where a contractual duty is exceeded

KEY CASE

***Hartley* v *Ponsonby* (1857) 7 E & B 872**

Concerning: consideration; exceeding an existing contractual duty

Facts

The facts of this case are very similar to *Stilk* v *Myrick* and involved a number of sailors deserting a ship. The captain had promised to pay the remaining sailors additional wages for crewing his ship back home. However, in *Stilk* v *Myrick,* 9 crew out of 11 remained; in this case 19 out of 36 remained.

Legal principle

The promise to pay was enforceable: the court considered that the greater proportional reduction in crew numbers (in this case almost half the crew deserted, rather than 2 from 11) made the return voyage much more dangerous since the ship was short-handed. The sailors' promise to return under more dangerous conditions had exceeded their existing contractual obligations and therefore this represented good consideration for the promise of extra pay.

Again, the principle appears to be that where a party does more than that for which they originally bargained, then this is good consideration to support a fresh bargain. This has also been applied in circumstances involving third parties.

Where there is an existing contractual duty owed to a third party

The performance (or promise to perform) an existing contractual duty owed by the promisee to a third party is also good consideration.

KEY CASE

Scotson v *Pegg* (1861) 6 H & N 295

Concerning: consideration; performance of an existing contractual duty owed to a third party

Facts

Scotson contracted to deliver coal to X, or to X's order. X sold the coal to Pegg and ordered Scotson to deliver the coal to Pegg. Pegg promised Scotson that he would unload it at a fixed daily rate. Pegg did not fulfil this promise. Scotson attempted to enforce Pegg's promise. Pegg argued that the promise was not binding because Scotson had not provided consideration as Scotson was bound by his contract with X (a third party) to deliver the coal.

Legal principle

It was held that delivery of the coal to Pegg (in other words, the performance of the existing contractual duty owed to X by Scotson) was good consideration to enforce Pegg's promise to pay.

The facts of *Scotson* v *Pegg* are best illustrated by a diagram (Figure 2.2).

Figure 2.2

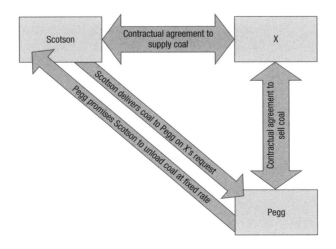

The decision in *Scotson* v *Pegg* has been approved by the Privy Council in *Pao On* v *Lau Yiu Long* [1980] AC 614 and *New Zealand Shipping Co Ltd* v *A.M. Satterthwaite & Co Ltd (The Eurymedon)* [1975] AC 154.

Where the rule in *Williams* v *Roffey* applies

The most recent 'refinement and limitation' to the rule in *Stilk* v *Myrick* was made in *Williams* v *Roffey Bros & Nicholls (Contractors) Ltd* [1991] 1 QB 1.

KEY CASE

Williams v Roffey Bros & Nicholls (Contractors) Ltd [1991] 1 QB 1

Concerning: consideration; extra benefit

Facts

Roffey Bros was a firm of builders contracted to renovate a block of flats. Their own contract contained a penalty clause for late completion, so it was in their interests to finish the work on time. They sub-contracted the carpentry work to Williams for £20,000. Williams fell behind schedule because, they claimed, they had not quoted a high enough price for the work. Roffey promised to pay Williams an additional sum of £10,300 to complete the carpentry on time. When the work was complete, Roffey refused to pay, claiming that the new agreement with Williams was void for lack of consideration (since Williams were already fulfilling a contractual obligation).

Legal principle

The Court of Appeal held that Williams had provided consideration by completing the work on time and therefore Roffey's promise to pay the additional £10,300 was binding, even though, at first glance, this proposition seemed incompatible with the rule from *Stilk* v *Myrick*.

Glidewell LJ explained that this case refined and limited the application of the principle from *Stilk* v *Myrick* but left the basic principle intact. Following *Ward* v *Byham* and *Pao On,* he stated that the present state of the law on this subject can be expressed in the following proposition:

(a) if A has entered into a contract with B to do work for, or to supply goods or services to, B in return for payment by B; and

(b) at some stage before A has completely performed his obligations under the contract B has reason to doubt whether A will, or will be able to, complete his side of the bargain; and

(c) B thereupon promises A an additional payment in return for A's promise to perform his contractual obligations on time; and

(d) as a result of giving his promise, B obtains in practice a benefit, or obviates a disbenefit; and

(e)   B's promise is not given as a result of economic duress or fraud on the part of A; then

(f)   the benefit to B is capable of being consideration for B's promise, so that the promise will be legally binding.

Following this proposition, the court considered that the practical benefit to Roffey was the avoidance of the penalty clause and, moreover, that the arrangement with Williams meant that they did not have to find another carpenter. This practical benefit was sufficient consideration for the promise to pay extra to Williams to complete what he was already bound to do under the existing contract.

> ✎ **EXAM TIP**
>
> If a problem question involves a situation where one party to a contractual agreement is desperate (for whatever reason) for the other party to complete their promise on time, then this is a good clue that a discussion of *Williams* v *Roffey* will be required.

Part payment of debt

The basic common law rule relating to part payment of a debt was stated in *Pinnel's Case*.

KEY CASE

Pinnel's Case (1602) 5 Co Rep 117a

Concerning: consideration; part payment of a debt

Facts

Cole owed Pinnel £8 10s. At Pinnel's request, Cole paid £5 2s. 6d. one month before the full sum was due. Cole claimed that there was an agreement that the part payment would discharge the full debt.

Legal principle

Pinnel was unsuccessful in claiming the balance of the unpaid debt. The court held that in general part payment of an original debt did not provide good consideration for the promise to waive the balance. However, since Pinnel gained some benefit by part payment having been made early, this was sufficient consideration to enforce his promise to forego the balance of the debt. The court stated that:

> Payment of a lesser sum on the day in satisfaction of a greater sum cannot be any satisfaction for the whole, because it appears to the Judges that by no possibility, a lesser sum can be a satisfaction to the [claimant] for a greater sum: but the gift of a horse, hawk, or robe, etc. in satisfaction is good . . . [as] more beneficial to the [claimant] than the money.

Therefore, payment of a lesser sum may discharge the full debt if some additional consideration is provided. This may be so if the part payment is made:

- before it is due (as in *Pinnel's Case*);
- by different means (for instance, if the creditor agrees to accept some property in lieu of money – even if this is worth less than the value of the debt: remember that consideration does not need to be adequate);
- in a different place to that originally specified.

These situations provide sufficient consideration in terms of a benefit to the creditor and a detriment to the debtor.

However, the rule from *Pinnel's Case* can operate harshly.

KEY CASE

Foakes v *Beer* (1884) 9 App Cas 605

Concerning: consideration; part payment of a debt

Facts

Foakes owed Beer £2,090. They agreed that Foakes could pay in instalments. Beer agreed that no further action would be taken if the debt was paid by the agreed date. Later, Beer demanded an additional interest payment. Foakes refused to pay.

Legal principle

Beer succeeded in the claim for the interest payment. The same reasoning was applied as in *Pinnel's Case*.

The decision in *Foakes* v *Beer* appears unfair to Foakes since he had relied on Beer's promise not to take further action if the debt was repaid. It is the potential harshness of the common law rule (which remains good law) that led to the development of the equitable doctrine of promissory estoppel.

Promissory estoppel

The equitable doctrine of promissory estoppel can provide a means of making a promise binding, even without consideration. It was developed from Lord Denning's *obiter* statement:

KEY CASE

Central London Property Trust v *High Trees House Ltd* [1947] KB 130

Concerning: promissory estoppel

Facts

In 1937 High Trees House Ltd leased a block of flats at the rate £2,500 per year from Central London Property Trust Ltd. Due to the war, occupancy rates were drastically lower than normal. In January 1940, the parties agreed in writing to reduce the rent by half. Neither party stipulated the period for which this reduced rent was to apply. High Trees paid the reduced rate for five years as the flats began to fill and by 1945 the flats were full. Central London Property Trust sued for payment of the full rental costs from July 1945 onwards.

Legal principle

The court considered *Hughes* v *Metropolitan Railway Co* (1877) 2 App Cas 439 which concerned the doctrine of waiver – that is, that parties should be prevented from going back on a promise to waive certain rights. In this case, Lord Denning held that the full rent was payable from the time that the flats became fully occupied in mid-1945. He also stated *obiter* that if Central London had tried to claim for the full rent from 1940 onwards, they would not have been able to. They would be estopped (i.e. prevented) from reneging on the promise upon which the defendants had relied as long as the circumstances which led to that promise continued.

Requirements for the doctrine to apply

The doctrine of promissory estoppel applies subject to certain requirements:

- there must be a clear or unequivocal promise or representation (*Collin* v *Duke of Westminster* [1985] QB 581);
- which is intended to affect the legal relationship between the parties (*Spence* v *Shell* (1980) 256 EG 819); and
- which indicates that the promisor will not insist upon his strict legal rights against the promisee in relation to the promise;
- the promise or representation must have influenced the conduct of the promisee in some way (it is often said that the promisee must have acted in reliance upon that promise) (*W J Alan Co Ltd* v *El Nasr Export and Import Co* [1972] 2 QB 189);
- it must be inequitable for the promisor to go back on the promise (*D & C Builders* v *Rees* [1965] 2 QB 617);
- the doctrine can only be used as a defence. Since it is an equitable doctrine, the general equitable maxim that 'equity is a shield, not a sword' applies. It does not create new rights (*Combe* v *Combe* [1951] 2 KB 215);

- the doctrine temporarily suspends rights; it does not extinguish them (*Tool Metal Manufacturing Co* v *Tungsten Electric Co Ltd* [1955] 1 WLR 761);
- since it is an equitable doctrine, it is available only at the discretion of the court.

In *Collier* v *P. & M.J. Wright (Holdings) Ltd* [2008] 1 WLR 643, Wright Ltd obtained a judgment for £50,000 against three partners, including Collier. Each of these partners was jointly and severally liable for the whole debt. Wright Ltd allegedly agreed to accept one-third of the sum due from each. Collier paid his instalment. The other two partners declared bankruptcy and Wright Ltd then attempted to enforce the whole judgment against Collier. In preliminary proceedings to determine whether there was a 'genuine triable issue' or a 'real prospect of success', the Court of Appeal held that Collier might have a case in promissory estoppel but reaffirmed the rule in *Pinnel's Case* that part payment of a debt cannot discharge the debt if unsupported by further consideration.

Arden LJ commented that:

> The facts of this case demonstrate that, if (1) a debtor offers to pay part only of the amount he owes; (2) the creditor voluntarily accepts that offer; and (3) in reliance on the creditor's acceptance the debtor pays that part of the amount he owes in full, the creditor will, by virtue of the doctrine of promissory estoppel, be bound to accept that sum in full and final satisfaction of the whole debt. For him to resile will of itself be inequitable. In addition, in these circumstances, the promissory estoppel has the effect of extinguishing the creditor's right to the balance of the debt. This part of our law originated in the brilliant obiter dictum of Denning J in the High Trees case [1947] KB 130. To a significant degree it achieves in practical terms the recommendation of the Law Revision Committee chaired by Lord Wright MR in 1937.

However, Longmore LJ obviously doubted that the promise would be clear enough when the substantial issue came to be tried and, in relation to the issue of whether it would be inequitable to allow the promisor to resile from his promise he said, 'There might . . . be much to be said on the other side'.

It appears unlikely that the doctrine will be developed further. In *Brikom Investments* v *Carr* [1979] QB 467 Roskill LJ stated that 'it would be wrong to extend the doctrine of promissory estoppel . . . to the extent of abolishing in this back-handed way the doctrine of consideration': in particular, an attempt to rely on *Williams* v *Roffey* in situations involving part payment of debt failed (*Re Selectmove* [1995] 2 All ER 531). You might find it helpful to read around this topic to develop your understanding. Halliwell's (1994) article provides a detailed analysis of the role of estoppel that would help you to prepare for an essay on this topic. Trukhtanov's (2008) article criticises the willingness to apply the equitable doctrine of promissory estoppel evident in *Collier*.

■ Putting it all together

Answer guidelines

See the sample question at the start of the chapter.

Approaching the question

This question requires you to discuss the situations in which promissory estoppel can prevent the enforcement of legal rights. This will require you to explain the relationship between the doctrine of promissory estoppel and analyse the role of consideration in the part payment of a debt.

Important points to include

- You could start by explaining the common law rule from *Pinnel's Case* – that part payment of a debt on the due date can never satisfy the full debt owed, but if some additional consideration is given then this may render a promise to forego the balance binding. You could mention *Foakes* v *Beer* and *Re Selectmove* in support of this.

- You should explain that the common law rule can lead to harsh outcomes and the doctrine of promissory estoppel was developed in order to mitigate some of the harshness of the common law.

- You should discuss the origins of the doctrine from *Hughes* v *Metropolitan Railway* and its development by Lord Denning in *High Trees*.

- You should also discuss, with supporting case authority, the conditions which must be satisfied for the doctrine to operate.

- Finally, you should draw together the various strands of your argument to reach a conclusion. In summary, the doctrine of promissory estoppel will prevent the enforcement of strict legal rights in certain circumstances, provided that the criteria required for its operation are met.

 Make your answer stand out

- As with many areas of contract law, this particular topic is heavily based on case law. You should therefore endeavour to support as many statements of law with case authority as you can. ▶

- You must take care to answer the question asked, rather than writing all you know about promissory estoppel. Take time and care to relate the points that you make back to the question that is asked. This will maintain focus.

- In a question of this nature, many students forget to discuss that promissory estoppel is an equitable doctrine: therefore, it is available only at the discretion of the court and may be used only as 'a shield, not a sword'. A discussion of the doctrine's equitable nature will demonstrate good understanding.

READ TO IMPRESS

Halliwell, M. (1994) Estoppel: unconscionability as a cause of action. *Legal Studies,* 14: 15.

Hooley, R. (1991) Consideration and the existing duty. *Journal of Business Law,* 19.

Steyn, J. (1997) Contract law: fulfilling the reasonable expectations of honest men. *Law Quarterly Review,* 110: 433.

Trukhtanov, A. (2008) *Foakes* v *Beer*: reform of the common law at the expense of equity. *Law Quarterly Review,* 124: 364.

www.pearsoned.co.uk/lawexpress

Go online to access more revision support including quizzes to test your knowledge, sample questions with answer guidelines, podcasts you can download, and more!

Contracts and third parties

3

Revision checklist

Essential points you should know:

- [ ] The operation of the general doctrine of privity of contract
- [ ] The various exceptions to the general doctrine of privity
- [ ] The circumstances in which a third party to a contract may recover damages
- [ ] The main provisions of the Contracts (Rights of Third Parties) Act 1999 and their effects
- [ ] The remedies that are available to a third party under the Contracts (Rights of Third Parties) Act 1999

Topic map

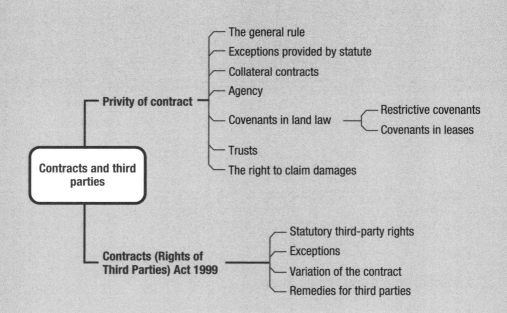

Contracts and third parties

Privity of contract
- The general rule
- Exceptions provided by statute
- Collateral contracts
- Agency
- Covenants in land law
  - Restrictive covenants
  - Covenants in leases
- Trusts
- The right to claim damages

Contracts (Rights of Third Parties) Act 1999
- Statutory third-party rights
- Exceptions
- Variation of the contract
- Remedies for third parties

A printable version of this topic map is available from **www.pearsoned.co.uk/lawexpress**

■ Introduction

In some situations, third parties to contracts may still acquire rights and liabilities under them, even if they are not party to the agreement themselves.

This chapter will start with the basic principle: that third parties may not enforce the terms of a contract to which they are not a party. However, there are many exceptions to the basic doctrine of privity of contract which have attempted to mitigate some of the potentially harsh outcomes that might result from its strict application. Once the position at common law has been investigated, the chapter will finally turn to consider the statutory reform of the area introduced by the Contracts (Rights of Third Parties) Act 1999 and will describe the effect of its most significant provisions.

ASSESSMENT ADVICE

Essay questions

Essay questions on privity often arise since the topic has a relatively unsatisfactory common law position which has resulted in both the development of a large number of common law exceptions and statutory reforms. Such questions will require a comprehensive knowledge and understanding of the various exceptions, the cases in which they arose and some of the underlying reasons as to why the courts decided to deviate from the general position in each case. You should also ensure that you are familiar with the key provisions of the Contracts (Rights of Third Parties) Act 1999, both in terms of their operation and the effect that they might have had on earlier cases if the Act had been in force at the time.

Problem questions

Problem questions which deal solely with privity are probably quite unlikely to arise. However, it is the sort of topic that could be mixed in with other areas of contract law and therefore a good working knowledge of the operation of this area is important. Even though the Contracts (Rights of Third Parties) Act 1999 is now in force, do not be tempted to discount the value of the common law position. You may be asked to advise one of the parties as to their position at common law as well as under statute, or be given a set of facts to discuss with a part question asking you if your answer would be any different if the events in the problem scenario took place before the Act was in force.

■ Sample question

Could you answer this question? Below is a typical essay question that could arise on this topic. Guidelines on answering the question are included at the end of the chapter, while a sample problem question and guidance on tackling it can be found on the companion website.

ESSAY QUESTION

Where a contract confers a benefit on a third party, it is enforceable by the third party in their own right. Discuss.

■ Privity of contract

The general rule

The general rule of privity of contract is that only parties to a contract can acquire rights and liabilities under that contract. It follows that if you are not a party to a contract then you cannot sue upon it, or be sued under it.

KEY CASE

Dunlop v *Selfridge* [1915] AC 847

Concerning: privity of contract

Facts

Dunlop sold tyres to Dew & Co who were wholesalers. Dew & Co undertook (expressly in the contract) that the manufacturers could fix the lowest price at which they could sell the tyre and promised not to sell the tyres below that price. Dew & Co also agreed to obtain the same pricing terms from customers to whom they resold the tyres. They sold tyres to Selfridge on these terms. Selfridge broke the pricing agreement and sold the tyres at discount prices. Dunlop sued Selfridge and sought an injunction to prevent them from selling their tyres at a discount.

Legal principle

Dunlop failed. Although there was a contract between them and Dew & Co, Selfridge were not a party to that contract and Dunlop, therefore, could not impose their terms upon them.

📖 **REVISION NOTE**

Dunlop v *Selfridge* also contained Lord Dunedin's approval of Pollock's definition of consideration (see Chapter 2).

In questions involving privity, it is often useful to sketch out a diagram showing where the various contractual relationships lie. For example, *Dunlop* v *Selfridge* could be depicted as shown in Figure 3.1.

Figure 3.1

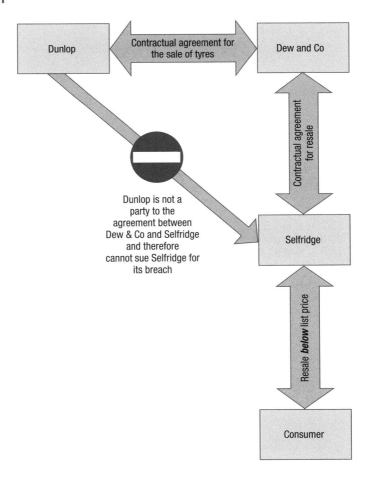

📖 **REVISION NOTE**

Tweddle v *Atkinson,* which was covered in Chapter 2, also involved privity of contract. Here the attempt by the third party to enforce the contract which conferred a benefit upon him failed on the rule of privity as well as failing for lack of consideration.

The common law rule of privity has been criticised for leading to harsh and unfair outcomes, particularly in cases where the contract purports to confer a benefit on a **third party** who remains unable to sue if that benefit is not forthcoming due to a breach by one of the parties to the contract (this was the situation in *Tweddle* v *Atkinson*). Therefore, a number of exceptions to the basic rule have been developed:

■ exceptions provided by statute
■ collateral contracts
■ agency
■ covenants in land law
■ trusts.

 Make your answer stand out

The basic doctrine of privity has been criticised in a number of cases. Look at the judgments in *Beswick* v *Beswick* [1968] AC 58, *Jackson* v *Horizon Holidays Ltd* [1975] 1 WLR 1468 and *Woodar Investment Development Ltd* v *Wimpey Construction (UK) Ltd* [1980] 1 WLR 277. In 1991 a Law Commission Consultation Paper (No. 121) also supported the argument for reform of the privity rule. In *Darlington Borough Council* v *Wiltshier Northern Limited* [1995] 1 WLR 68 Lord Steyn commented:

There is no doctrinal, logical or policy reason why the law should deny effectiveness to a contract for the benefit of a third party where that is the expressed intention of the parties.

If you summarise the judicial criticisms within these cases, you will acquire the depth of knowledge which would come in useful for an essay question on privity.

Exceptions provided by statute

Statutory exceptions to the rule include the following:

Statutory provision	Effect
Section 148(7), Road Traffic Act 1988	Requires drivers to have third-party insurance which can be relied upon by third parties who suffer loss or damage even though they are not a party to that contract
Section 11, Married Women's Property Act 1882	Allows a wife to claim on her husband's life assurance policy
Section 29, Bills of Exchange Act 1882	A third party may sue on a cheque or bill of exchange
Section 136, Law of Property Act 1925	Allows rights arising under a contract to be assigned to a third party
Section 56(1), Law of Property Act 1925	Allows a person to acquire an interest in land or other property or the benefit of a covenant relating to land or other property even if that person is not expressly named in the conveyance (or other document)
Competition Act 1998	Prohibits price-fixing arrangements (such as those in *Dunlop* v *Selfridge*)

However, attempts to use statute as a creative 'loophole' to avoid the basic doctrine of privity have failed (see, for example, *Beswick* v *Beswick,* which concerned the use of section 56(1) of the Law of Property Act 1925 in relation to personal property rather than to land or an interest in land).

Collateral contracts

A collateral contract may be used to avoid the rule relating to privity. In essence a contract between two parties may be accompanied by a collateral contract between one of those parties and a third party *relating to the same subject matter.*

KEY CASE

Shanklin Pier v *Detel Products Ltd* [1951] AC 847

Concerning: privity of contract, collateral contracts

Facts

The claimants entered into a contract with painting contractors to paint their pier, having been assured by the defendants (paint manufacturers) that their paint would last for at least seven years without deterioration. The defendants then sold the paint to the contractors. However, the paint peeled within three months. The pier owners could not sue the painters since they had carried out the work professionally and thus had completed their side of the contract. The pier owners sued the paint manufacturers.

Legal principle

The pier owners were successful. Although they were not a party to the contract between the paint manufacturers and the painting contractors (and therefore there was no privity of contract), it was held that a collateral contract had arisen from their promise as to the suitability of the paint.

The collateral contract device can be seen as a way to identify a contract between the party making a promise (Detel) and the other party (Shanklin Pier) since this promise has induced the other party (Shanklin Pier) to enter into a separate contract with a different party (the painting contractors). Therefore, the party making the promise (Detel) gains some benefit in being able to sell their goods (paint) on the strength of the 'main' contract (between Shanklin Pier and the painting contractors) and are held to be bound by their promise (see Figure 3.2).

Figure 3.2

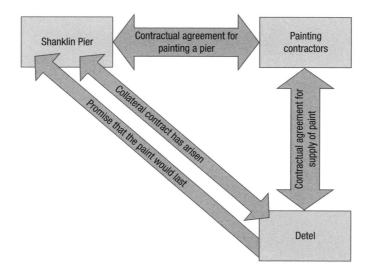

Strictly speaking, the use of a collateral contract is not an exception to the doctrine of privity, since a new contract arises. However, it is an effective means of evading the doctrine of privity.

Agency

The contract of agency is a common law exception to the doctrine of privity. The parties in an agency arrangement are as follows:

Party	Description
Principal	The party on whose behalf the contract is made and who receives the benefit arising under the contract.
Agent	The agent is a party to the contract with the third party. The agent has a direct contractual relationship with the third party, but is making the contract on behalf of the principal and not on his own behalf.
Third party	The third party enters into the contract with the agent. However, the rules of agency provide that there is no contractual relationship with the agent. Instead the principal is bound by the contractual relationship with the third party which has been entered into by the agent on his behalf.

The relationship between these three parties can be depicted as shown in Figure 3.3.

Figure 3.3

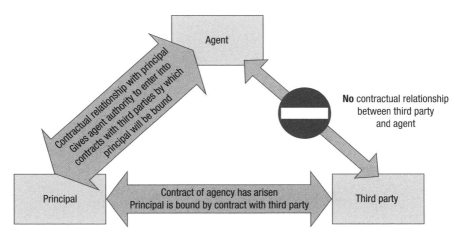

Covenants in land law

A covenant is an agreement between two or more parties made in the form of a deed. It is therefore similar to a contract, with the exception that contracts made by deed do not have to be supported by consideration.

📖 **REVISION NOTE**

This section covers only the very basic details of land law sufficient to illustrate the points relating to privity of contract. If you have already studied land law, it might be useful to look back at your material on restrictive covenants and leases to refresh your memory on the principles before proceeding to cover the rest of this section.

Restrictive covenants

In land law, in certain circumstances, covenants can 'run with the land'. If, for example, Tom, a builder, builds a row of houses, and sells them to Chris, Becky and Tricia, he can enter into a covenant with each of them in which they promise not to block the shared drains. However, if Becky sells her house to Sanjay, then Sanjay and Tom are not parties to any contract. Therefore, if Sanjay blocks the shared drain, under the doctrine of privity, Tom could not sue Sanjay because they are not parties to the covenant (contract). Chris and Tricia also have no contractual relationship with Sanjay, even though they are suffering from blocked drains as a result of his actions.

In order to address this situation, an equitable device has developed which means that *restrictive covenants* (promises to refrain from doing something) will, if properly created, bind successive purchasers of the land even though there is no privity between them and the original seller.

KEY CASE

Tulk v *Moxhay* (1848) 41 ER 1143

Concerning: privity of contract; restrictive covenants over land

Facts

Tulk owned land which he sold subject to an express promise that it would not be used for property development. The land was resold several times, subject to the same undertaking. Moxhay eventually bought the land and, despite knowing of the restriction, intended to build upon it. Tulk sought an injunction to prevent Moxhay from building on the land.

Legal principle

Tulk's claim was successful. The court considered that it would be unconscionable for Moxhay to buy with knowledge of the restriction and yet to build on the land. An injunction was therefore granted to enforce the original agreement between Tulk and the first purchaser of the land, even though Moxhay had not been a party to that agreement.

This principle applies subject to two conditions:

- the third party must have had notice of the restrictive covenant at the time of purchase; and
- the original seller must have retained land which was capable of benefiting from the restriction.

However, the principle from *Tulk* v *Moxhay* generally applies only to land. It certainly failed in relation to a price-fixing arrangement (similar to that in *Dunlop* v *Selfridge*) in *Taddy* v *Sterious* [1904] 1 Ch 354. However, in *Lord Strathcona Steamship Co* v *Dominion Coal Co* [1926] AC 108, the Privy Council applied the principle in relation to the use of a ship that had been sold with notice of a charter. This decision was criticised on the basis that the third party did not have any proprietary interest as required by *Tulk* v *Moxhay* and its use has been restricted since. In *Clore* v *Theatrical Properties Ltd* [1936] 3 All ER 483 it was held that the decision in *Strathcona* should be used only in the particular circumstances relating to ships' charters. *Port Line Ltd* v *Ben Line Steamers Ltd* [1958] 2 QB 146 went further in stating that *Strathcona* was wrongly decided.

Covenants in leases

Where a landlord grants a lease to another person, there are typically various covenants contained within the lease. There is privity of contract between the landlord and tenant and the terms of the lease are enforceable by both. The landlord may also enforce those covenants against anyone to whom the lease is assigned (sold). Sections 141 and 142 of the Law of Property Act 1925 also provide that a tenant may be able to enforce covenants against a new landlord (if the freehold is sold) and vice versa that the new landlord may enforce those covenants against the tenant. However, if the lessee sub-lets the property, the landlord will have no privity with the sub-tenant (see Figure 3.4).

Figure 3.4

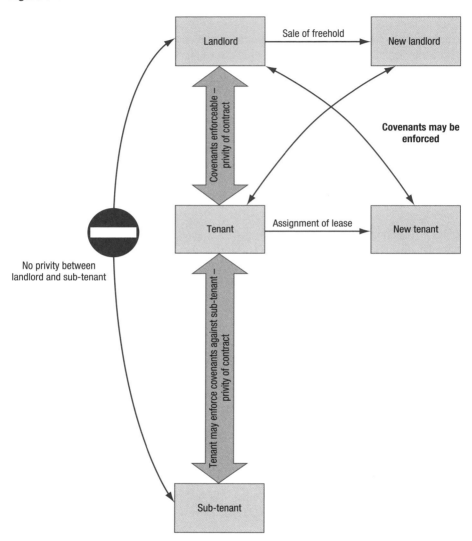

📖 **REVISION NOTE**

As with the previous section on land law, this section carries limited discussion of the fundamentals of trusts. If you have already studied equity and trusts, you should take some time to re-equip yourself with the basics before looking at the specific application of trusts to privity in the rest of this section.

Trusts

The doctrine of privity may also be avoided in the situation where one of the parties to a contract which confers a benefit on a third party holds their contractual rights in trust for that third party. This can be depicted as shown in Figure 3.5.

This principle was established in *Gregory & Parker* v *Williams* (1817) 3 Mer 582 and affirmed in *Les Affrêteurs Réunis SA* v *Walford* [1919] AC 801. In order for the principle to apply, there must be an express intention in the contract between A and B that C should receive a benefit, and a trust will be found only if the court considers that the interest is compatible with the general principles of trust law (*Green* v *Russell* [1959] 2 QB 226).

Figure 3.5

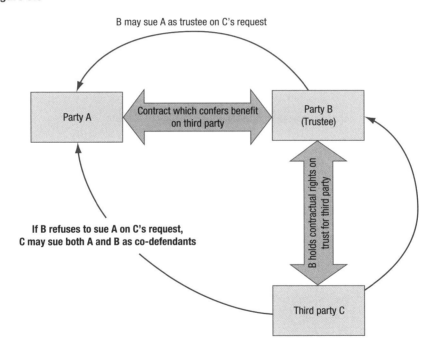

REVISION NOTE

Remember that the use of trusts in an attempt to circumvent the doctrine of privity is a creation of the law of trusts rather than the law of contract. It is included here to demonstrate how creative parties have had to become in order to find ways around seemingly harsh and rigid applications of the basic doctrine.

The right to claim damages

Unless one of the exceptions to the doctrine of privity arises, then the third party has no means of enforcing the contract at common law unless one of the parties to the contract sues in their own right. However, if the contract confers a benefit on the third party, it is unlikely that the party who brings the claim will have suffered loss themselves. Therefore, if an award of **damages** is made, strictly speaking, this will be to compensate the party who brings the claim, who – having suffered no loss – would be entitled to only nominal damages.

📖 REVISION NOTE

The remedy of nominal damages is discussed further in Chapter 9.

However, there is a common law rule originating from the shipping case of *Dunlop* v *Lambert* (1839) 7 ER 824 which allows a remedy to be awarded to a party even without privity of contract 'where no other would be available to a person sustaining loss which under a rational legal system ought to be compensated by the person who caused it'.

This rule was applied broadly in relation to a family holiday.

KEY CASE

Jackson v *Horizon Holidays Ltd* **[1975] 1 WLR 1468**

Concerning: privity of contract: recovery by third parties

Facts

Jackson had booked a family holiday in his sole name. For a variety of reasons, the holiday was a complete travesty: the accommodation, food, services, facilities and general standard of the hotel to which they were transported proved so unsatisfactory that the whole family suffered discomfort, vexation, inconvenience and distress and went home disappointed. Jackson sued the holiday company on his own behalf and that of his family. The company disputed that it should pay damages in respect of the family since it was not a party to the contract.

Legal principle

The Court of Appeal held that the disappointment suffered by the family was a loss to Jackson himself and awarded damages in respect of the whole family on that basis.

This decision was criticised as being of too wide an application and was narrowed by the House of Lords.

KEY CASE

Woodar Investment Development Ltd v *Wimpey Construction (UK) Ltd* **[1980] 1 WLR 277**

Concerning: privity of contract: recovery by third parties

Facts

The purchasers, Wimpey Construction, had entered into a contract to buy certain land from the vendors, Woodar. The purchase price was £850,000 of which £150,000 was to be paid on completion to Transworld Trade, a third party. The sale was to complete within two months of planning permission for the site being granted or a fixed date (whichever was the earlier). Wimpey unlawfully repudiated the contract after the market fell.

Legal principle

The issue here concerned whether damages should include the £150,000 payable to the third party. Although the House of Lords did not overrule *Jackson,* it was held that there was no general principle allowing a party to a contract to sue on behalf of a third party who had suffered loss as a result of breach of that contract.

It appeared, then, that the relaxation of the doctrine was not of general utility and that its use had been specifically restricted by the House of Lords to holiday contracts. However, the principle from *Dunlop* v *Lambert* was extended to property as well as carriage of goods in *Linden Gardens Trust Ltd* v *Lanesta Sludge Disposals Ltd* [1994] AC 85 and more recently considered (although not clarified) by the House of Lords in *Alfred McAlpine Construction Ltd* v *Panatown Ltd.*

KEY CASE

Alfred McAlpine Construction Ltd v *Panatown Ltd* **[2001] 1 AC 518**

Concerning: privity of contract: recovery by third parties

Facts

There was a contract between McAlpine and Panatown for the design and build of a multi-storey car park. McAlpine had also entered into a 'duty of care' deed with Unex Investment Properties Ltd (UIPL), which was the owner of the site. By that deed UIPL acquired a direct remedy against McAlpine in respect of any failure by the contractor to exercise reasonable skill, care and attention to any matter within the scope of the contractor's responsibilities under the contract. The deed was expressly assignable by the owner to its successors in title. Serious defects were found in the building and Panatown sued.

Legal principle

The House of Lords held that the duty of care deed with the third party (UIPL) prevented Panatown from suing since this deed gave the third party a specific remedy. However, the Lords were split 3–2 on the issue, which suggests that the law is still somewhat unclear in this area.

The common law position was amended by statute in the form of the Contracts (Rights of Third Parties) Act 1999.

■ Contracts (Rights of Third Parties) Act 1999

As you have seen, there are a number of exceptions to the general doctrine of privity of contract. This suggests that the courts have been far from content with the strict operation of the doctrine. The increasing number of exceptions led to this area of law becoming more complicated, and it is not surprising that there have been several calls for legislative reform. Following a Law Commission consultation, a draft Bill was presented to Parliament which ultimately became the Contracts (Rights of Third Parties) Act 1999.

Statutory third-party rights

The main changes to the common law position are found in section 1 of the Act.

KEY STATUTE

Contracts (Rights of Third Parties) Act 1999, section 1(1)–(3)

1.– (1) Subject to the provisions of this Act, a person who is not a party to a contract (a 'third party') may in his own right enforce a term of the contract if –

(a) the contract expressly provides that he may, or

(b) subject to subsection (2), the term purports to confer a benefit on him.

(2) Subsection (1)(b) does not apply if on a proper construction of the contract it appears that the parties did not intend the term to be enforceable by the third party.

> (3) The third party must be expressly identified in the contract by name, as a member of a class or as answering a particular description but need not be in existence when the contract is entered into.

Therefore, the Act allows contractual provisions to be enforced by a non-contracting party in two circumstances:

- where the contract expressly provides that he may (section 1(1)(a));
- where the contract term purports to confer a benefit upon him (section 1(1)(b));
- provided that it appears that the parties did not intend the term not to be enforceable by the third party (section 1(2)).

In *Nisshin Shipping Co Ltd* v *Cleaves & Co Ltd* [2004] 1 All ER (Comm) 481 the interpretation of the Act was tested in court for the first time. It was held that if the contract is neutral on the question of whether the term was intended to be enforceable by the third party, then section 1(2) does not disapply section 1(1)(b).

In *Dolphin & Maritime & Aviation Services Ltd v Sveriges Angfartygs Assurans Forening (The Swedish Club)* [2009] EWHC 716 (Comm), Christopher Clark J drew a distinction between contracts which have a purpose of conferring a benefit and those which have a benefit as an incidental effect:

> A contract does not purport to confer a benefit on a third party simply because the position of that third party will be improved if the contract is performed. The reference in the section to the term purporting to 'confer' a benefit seems to me to connote that the language used by the parties shows that one of the purposes of their bargain (rather than one of the incidental effects if performed) was to benefit the third party.

Section 1(3) provides that the party must be identified by name, as a member of a class or answering a particular description but need not exist when the contract is entered into. This could extend rights to unborn children, a future spouse or a company which was not incorporated at the time of formation of the contract.

In *Great Eastern Shipping Co Ltd* v *Far East Chartering Ltd (The Jag Ravi)* [2012] EWCA Civ 180, the court permitted successful reliance on section 1 where a letter of indemnity was held to be capable of being accepted by a ship-owner as the agent of the charterer.

Exceptions

The Act will not apply to:

- bills of exchange, promissory notes and negotiable instruments (section 6(1));
- statutory contracts that were made under section 14 of the Companies Act 1985 (now repealed by the Companies Act 2006) (section 6(2));

- any incorporation document of a limited liability partnership or any limited liability partnership agreement (section 6(2A));
- contracts of employment (section 6(3));
- contracts for the carriage of goods by sea (other than clauses of exclusion or limitation) (section 6(4)).

Variation of the contract

The promised benefit to the third party may not be removed by a variation of the contract if:

- the third party has communicated his assent to the term to the promisor (section 2(1)(a));
- the promisor is aware that the third party has relied on the term (section 2(1)(b)); or
- the promisor can reasonably be expected to have foreseen that the third party would rely on the term and the third party has in fact relied on it (section 2(1)(c)).

Remedies for third parties

Section 1(5) of the Act provides that the third party has available to him any remedy that would have been available to him in an action for breach of contract if he had been a party to the contract. The rules relating to damages, injunctions, specific performance and other relief apply in the same way as if he had been a party to the contract. However, if the promisee has already recovered damages from the promisor in respect of losses suffered by the third party, then section 5 will operate to reduce any award to the third party to take account of damages already recovered from the promisor. This provision operates to prevent the promisor from double liability to both the promisee and the third party.

■ Putting it all together

Answer guidelines

See the sample question at the start of the chapter.

Approaching the question

This is an essay question that requires you to examine the extent to which contracts which confer benefits on third parties are enforceable by those third parties. As such, you should realise that it requires a discussion of contracts and third parties starting from the basic notion of privity of contract and moving on to explore the situations in which the law has moved away from the strict position and why that has happened.

Important points to include

- You should provide a brief description of the doctrine of privity, explaining that the doctrine derives from *Tweddle* v *Atkinson* and *Dunlop* v *Selfridge.*
- You could then go on to discuss criticisms of this aspect of the doctrine (*Beswick* v *Beswick*; *Woodar* v *Wimpey*; *Darlington* v *Wiltshier*).
- Note how courts have developed exceptions (*Jackson* v *Horizon Holidays*).
- Note briefly that a number of statutory exceptions exist.
- Explain that the Contracts (Rights of Third Parties) Act 1999 has reformed the doctrine of privity.
- Explain that the two main provisions of the Act apply to most contracts. The parties to the contract can give rights to third parties in two ways (section 1): (1) contract expressly provides that the third party may enforce the term; (2) where the term of the contract purports to confer a benefit on the third party.
- Explain why the second limb is more problematic – difficulties in interpretation (but note *Nisshin Shipping*); where more than one term for benefit of the third party each term will have to satisfy the test.

Make your answer stand out

- When using *Tweddle* to illustrate the fact that a third party cannot enforce a promise made for his benefit you could also link this to the point that the contract would fail for lack of consideration (see Chapter 2).
- A good answer would also refer to the Law Commission's criticisms of the doctrine as well as the judicial criticism in case law.
- When considering exceptions, the more relevant case examples you include, the better supported your answer will be (*Linden Gardens Trust Darlington* v *Wiltshier*; *Alfred McAlpine Construction Ltd* v *Panatown*).
- You could demonstrate your depth of understanding by briefly referring to agency, assignment and trusts as means of avoiding the doctrine.
- In relation to the Contracts (Rights of Third Parties) Act 1999 a good answer would note that the third party does not become a party to the contract, that the parties to the contract may expressly state that the Act does not apply in ▶

whole or part to the contract, and that the parties to the contract may vary and rescind the third party's rights but only with the third party's consent in three situations.

■ A very good answer would briefly consider how past cases might be decided now: look at *Tweddle* v *Atkinson* and *Beswick* v *Beswick*. Note also *Dunlop* v *Selfridge* where the contractual burden still cannot be imposed.

READ TO IMPRESS

Andrews, N. (2001) Strangers to justice no longer: the reversal of the privity rule under the Contracts (Rights of Third Parties) Act 1999. *Cambridge Law Journal,* 60: 353.

Burrows, A. (2000) The Contracts (Rights of Third Parties) Act and its implications for commercial contracts. *Lloyd's Maritime and Commercial Law Quarterly,* 540.

MacMillan, C. (2000) A birthday present for Lord Denning: the Contracts (Rights of Third Parties) Act 1999. *Modern Law Review,* 63: 721.

Rawlings, P. (2006) Third party rights in contract. *Lloyd's Maritime and Commercial Law Quarterly,* 7.

Smith, S. (1997) Contracts for the benefit of third parties: in defence of the third-party rule. *Oxford Journal of Legal Studies,* 7: 643.

www.pearsoned.co.uk/lawexpress

 Go online to access more revision support including quizzes to test your knowledge, sample questions with answer guidelines, podcasts you can download, and more!

Contractual terms

4

Revision checklist

Essential points you need to know:

☐ The distinction between a representation and a term of the contract and the consequences of the distinction

☐ The difference between express and implied contract terms

☐ The way in which terms are implied into a contract under common law

☐ The operation of statutory implied terms

Topic map

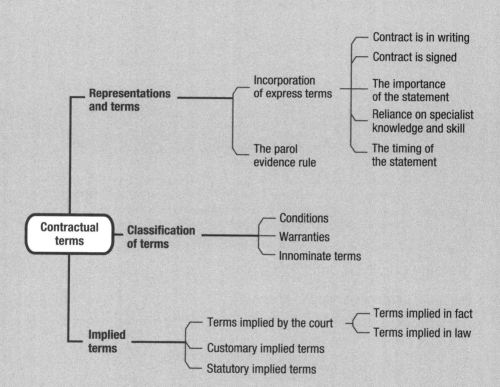

■ Introduction

Contracts are made up of contractual terms.

While the majority of these are expressly agreed by the parties entering into the contract, contracts may also include terms that are not expressly stated but are implied to give effect to the intention of the parties, or implied by custom or by law.

This chapter will begin by looking at the different types of pre-contractual statements, the means by which they may be incorporated into the contract and an indication of the remedies that may be available in the event of their breach. It will then move on to consider the classification of contractual terms into conditions, warranties and innominate terms and examine each of these in respect of their relative importance and the consequent action that may be taken if they are breached. Finally, the chapter will look at the role of implied terms, with particular reference to the terms implied into consumer contracts by statute.

ASSESSMENT ADVICE

Essay questions

Essay questions on contractual terms could concentrate on one area of the topic in particular or a much broader-ranging discussion of the means by which terms are incorporated into contracts. Such essay questions would tend to be unpopular with students as the operation of contractual terms is often either overlooked in selective revision or skimmed just in case the topic comes up as part of a problem question. This means that if you are equipped with a good understanding of contractual terms, then you would be well placed for your answer to stand out from those done by students who are attempting the question as a last resort. Remember that unpopular questions tend to be done either very well, or very badly.

Problem questions

Problem questions on contractual terms are often mixed with other topics. It is particularly common to find questions relating to the existence or incorporation of contract terms in connection with issues relating to the exclusion of contractual liability – especially in relation to contracts for the sale of goods (Chapter 5) or remedies for breach (Chapter 9). While it would be relatively unusual to encounter a problem question that dealt exclusively with contractual terms as far as they are covered in this chapter, you will need to understand them well enough so as not to miss out on the marks that will be available for discussing them in the context of a problem question.

Sample question

Could you answer this question? Below is a typical essay question that could arise on this topic. Guidelines on answering the question are included at the end of the chapter, while a sample problem question and guidance on tackling it can be found on the companion website.

> **ESSAY QUESTION**
>
> The contents of a contract are not always written within it.
>
> Discuss.

Representations and terms

Before a contract is formed, the parties will make various statements in the course of negotiation. Since these statements may form part of the contract, it is important to be able to distinguish between contractual terms and other statements. We must consider so-called '**puffs**', **representations** and **terms**.

> **KEY DEFINITIONS: Puff, representation, term**
>
> A '**puff**' is a boastful statement made in advertising.
>
> A **representation** is a statement that induces a party to enter into a contract (but does not form part of it).
>
> A **term** is a promise or undertaking that becomes part of the contract itself.

The distinction between these three types of statement is important as the legal consequences that result if a pre-contractual statement is false differ depending on the classification of the statement. This is so even though both representations and terms induced the formation of the contract. See Figure 4.1.

Figure 4.1

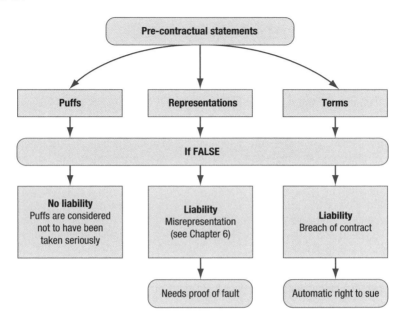

Incorporation of express terms

Given the distinction between the different types of pre-contractual statement, it follows that not all representations end up as terms of the contract. The distinction between representations and terms is generally decided by considering key questions:

- What was the intention of the parties?
- Were the statements intended to raise expectations which the contract should uphold?
- The question put forward by the House of Lords in *Heilbut, Symons & Co* v *Buckleton* [1913] AC 30 was as follows:

    Was there evidence of an intention by one or both parties that there should be a contractual liability in respect of the accuracy of the statement?

In order to answer these questions, there are a number of tests that the courts have developed.

Contract is in writing

If the contract is in writing, then the statements within it are usually regarded as terms rather than representations. It follows that statements that were made before the contract are considered to be mere representations (otherwise the parties would have reduced them to writing). The courts, however, will still consider the intention of the parties, in case they intended the contract to be partly in writing and partly oral.

KEY CASE

***J Evans and Son (Portsmouth) Ltd v Andrea Mezario Ltd* [1976] 1 WLR 1078**

Concerning: incorporation of terms

Facts

The claimants had contracted with the defendants to make the transport arrangements for the carriage of goods to England. A clause in the contract stated that the shipper 'reserves to itself complete freedom in respect of . . . the procedure to be followed in the handling and transportation of the goods'. However, there was a verbal agreement in which the defendants promised that they would transport the claimants' cargo below deck. Because of an oversight on the part of the defendants, a container was shipped to England on deck. The ship met a swell which caused the container to fall off the deck and the machine was lost overboard.

The claimants claimed damages against the defendants for the loss of the machine, alleging that the carriage of the container on deck had been a breach of the contract of carriage.

Legal principle

The court held that the oral promise was incorporated in the contract. Per Roskill LJ, the contract was partly oral, partly written and partly by conduct and in those circumstances the court was entitled to look at all the evidence to determine the bargain struck between the parties. It followed that the defendants were liable for breach of the oral promise.

Contract is signed

Where a written agreement is signed, the parties to it are considered to be in agreement with everything it contains *even if they have not read it.*

KEY CASE

***L'Estrange* v *Graucob* [1934] 2 KB 394**

Concerning: incorporation of terms; signed contract

Facts

Mrs L'Estrange owned a café. She ordered a cigarette machine from the manufacturers which was faulty. The contract, which she had signed, contained a clause stating that 'any express or implied condition, statement or warranty, statutory or otherwise not stated herein is hereby excluded'. L'Estrange claimed for breach of a term implied by the Sale of Goods Act 1893 that the goods were unfit for purpose. She also claimed that she had not seen the clause and therefore had no knowledge of its contents.

Legal principle

L'Estrange's claim failed. Scrutton LJ stated that:

> When a document containing contractual terms is signed, then, in the absence of fraud, or, I will add, misrepresentation, the party signing it is bound and it is wholly immaterial whether he has read the document or not.

📖 REVISION NOTE

Note that exclusions of liability for the terms implied by the Sale of Goods Act 1893 were allowed. This was not the case under the later Sale of Goods Act 1979. These terms would also now be governed by the Unfair Contract Terms Act 1977 or the Consumer Rights Act 2015 (depending on whether the contract in question is a 'consumer contract'). See Chapter 5.

The importance of the statement

The greater the importance attached to a particular statement by one party, the more likely it is to be considered to be a term. Therefore, if the party would not have entered into the contract if the statement had not been made, then that statement is highly likely to be considered a term – otherwise the contract would not be giving effect to the intention of the parties.

KEY CASE

Bannerman v *White* (1861) 10 CBNS 844

Concerning: incorporation of terms; importance of statement

Facts

The defendant was the purchaser of hops. Before the contract was formed the purchaser stated that 'if they have been treated with sulphur, I am not interested in even knowing the price of them'. The seller stated (wrongly) that they had not been so treated. When the purchaser discovered this, he repudiated the contract. The seller sued on the basis that the discussions were preliminary to the contract and not part of it.

Legal principle

The seller failed. The court held that the statement was so important to the purchaser that it became a term of the contract that had been breached.

This principle has also applied to an assurance that:

- a new house would be 'as good as the show house' (*Birch* v *Paramount Estates (Liverpool) Ltd* (1956) 16 EG 396); and
- a heifer (a young cow) had not been used for breeding (*Couchman* v *Hill* [1947] KB 554).

Reliance on specialist knowledge and skill

Where one party relies on a statement made with the specialist knowledge or skill of the other party in deciding whether or not to enter into a contract, then the statement may be considered to be a term of the contract.

KEY CASE

Dick Bentley Productions Ltd v *Harold Smith (Motors) Ltd* [1965] 1 WLR 623

Concerning: incorporation of terms; specialist knowledge

Facts

The claimant asked the defendants to source a 'well vetted' Bentley. The defendants claimed that a particular car had done 20,000 miles since being fitted with a new engine and gearbox. It had, in fact, done 100,000 miles, which the claimant discovered after purchasing the car.

Legal principle

The statement regarding mileage was held to be a term of the contract. The claimant had relied on the specialist knowledge of the dealer in making the statement which was a major factor in his decision to enter into the contract.

However, in a similar case where an erroneous (but honest) statement as to a vehicle's age was made by a private seller with no expertise or specialist skill, the statement was not considered to be a term of the contract (*Oscar Chess Ltd* v *Williams* [1956] 1 All ER 325) but a representation: the party to whom the statement was made was a car dealer and was therefore perfectly capable of determining the veracity of the statement for themselves.

The timing of the statement

Where there is a significant lapse in time between the statement made and the formation of the contract, the courts are more likely to consider the statement as a representation rather than as a term of the contract.

This view was also considered more recently in *Inntrepreneur Pub Co* v *East Crown Ltd* [2000] 2 Lloyd's Rep 611 in which it was stated that the longer the interval between the statement and the contract, 'the greater the presumption that the parties did not intend the statement to have contractual effect'.

KEY CASE

Routledge v *McKay* [1954] 1 WLR 615

Concerning: incorporation of terms; lapse of time

Facts

A motorcycle was first registered in 1939. A new registration document was issued which erroneously stated this as 1941. In 1949 the then owner, who was unaware of this inaccuracy, stated that the age of the motorcycle was 1941 to a prospective buyer. The buyer bought the motorcycle a week later by a written contract that did not stipulate the age of the motorcycle. He later discovered the true age and sued for breach of a term.

Legal principle

The buyer's claim failed. The court considered that the lapse of time was too great to infer that the contract was formed based on the statement of age and as such the statement was not incorporated as a term of the contract.

The parol evidence rule

The general 'parol evidence' rule states that where a contract has been reduced to writing, extrinsic evidence (whether written or oral) is inadmissible to add to, vary, or contradict its terms. In other words, at common law, a written contract is presumed to contain everything upon which the parties agreed and anything that is not embodied in the contract is considered never to have been intended to be included. This is so even if there is oral or written matter (such as earlier drafts of the contract or accompanying correspondence) which suggests otherwise.

The Law Commission (1976) recommended that the rule should be abolished, but by 1986 concluded that it did not stop the courts accepting parol evidence if this was consistent with the intention of the parties.

A number of exceptions to the basic rule have been developed:

- If the written agreement was not intended to be the whole contract on which the parties had actually agreed, parol evidence is admissible (*J. Evans and Son (Portsmouth) Ltd* v *Andrea Mezario Ltd*).
- Parol evidence may be given to determine the validity of the contract.
- Parol evidence can be used to show that the contract does not yet operate, or that it has ceased to operate (*Pym* v *Campbell* (1856) 6 E& 370).

- Parol evidence can be used to show in what capacities the parties contracted (*Humfrey* v *Dale* (1857) 7 E & B 266).
- Parol evidence can be used to explain words or phrases which are ambiguous, or which, if taken literally, make no sense.
- Parol evidence of custom is admissible 'to annex incidents to written contracts in matters with respect to which they are silent' (*Hutton* v *Warren* (1836) 1 M & W 466).
- Parol evidence may be used to show that the written document does not record the true agreement accurately, enabling the equitable remedy of rectification (*Webster* v *Cecil* (1861) 54 ER 812).
- Parol evidence can be used to show that the parties made two related contracts, one written and the other oral (i.e. a collateral contract) (*City & Westminster Properties* v *Mudd* [1959] Ch 129).

Classification of terms

Terms that are incorporated into a contract fall into three categories:

- conditions
- warranties
- innominate terms.

The distinction between these three types relates to their relative importance and the consequent action that can be taken in the event of their breach (see Figure 4.2).

Figure 4.2

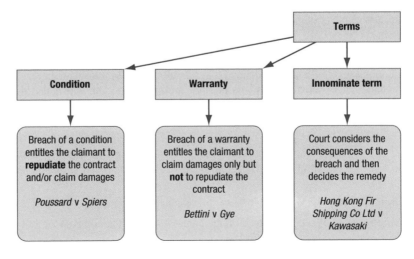

Conditions

A **condition** is said to 'go to the root' of the contract. Therefore, conditions are the most important terms of the contract. It follows that the breach of a condition would mean that something essential to the contract had failed and as such the contract could not feasibly continue.

Breach of a condition allows the claimant to access the full range of contractual remedies.

📖 **REVISION NOTE**

Remedies are covered in Chapter 9.

The injured claimant can sue for damages as well as repudiating his own obligations under the contract. In other words, the claimant can consider that his contractual obligations have ceased. Once discharged, he is free from the contract.

KEY CASE

Poussard v *Spiers and Pond* (1876) 1 QBD 410

Concerning: breach of condition

Facts

An actress was under contract to appear as the lead in an operetta. She was taken ill and unable to attend the first performances. Her role was given to her understudy. Once recovered, she sued for breach of contract.

Legal principle

The claim by the actress failed. The court held that as the lead performer she was of crucial importance to the success of the production. This was therefore a condition of the contract which she had breached by failing to attend the first performances. Therefore, the producers were entitled to repudiate and terminate the contract.

Warranties

A **warranty** is a contractual term of lesser importance than a condition. Since breach of a warranty is less significant than breach of a condition, the contract might be able to continue after such a breach. Since a warranty does not 'go to the root' of a contract, its breach is less likely to be fatal to the contract as a whole.

Therefore, the remedies available to a claimant who has suffered a breach of warranty are limited to damages only. The injured party does not have the same right to repudiate the contract and consider themselves discharged from it in the same way as they would for breach of a condition.

KEY CASE

Bettini v *Gye* (1876) 1 QBD 183

Concerning: breach of warranty

Facts

The facts of this case are similar to those of *Poussard* v *Spiers.* Here, a singer was under contract to appear in a series of concerts in different theatres. The contract included a term that he should attend rehearsals for six days before the live performances commenced. The singer did not attend the first three rehearsals. He was replaced. The singer sued for breach of contract.

Legal principle

The claim by the singer was successful. The court held that attendance at rehearsals was peripheral to the main purpose of the contract. Therefore the term was considered to be a warranty which entitled the producers to sue for damages but not to repudiate and terminate the contract by replacing the singer with another.

Just because a term is described in a contract as a condition does not mean that it is automatically a condition if its actual content is ancillary to the main purpose of the contract. It is the importance of the term that determines its classification, not the label that has been attached to it within the contract itself (*L. Schuler AG* v *Wickman Machine Tool Sales* [1974] 2 All ER 39).

Innominate terms

The classification of contractual terms as conditions or warranties is based upon a determination as to whether the parties to the contract intended the term in question to be classified as one or the other.

More recently, the courts have developed an approach involving so-called **innominate terms**. This is a 'wait and see' approach: in other words, the courts look at the effects of the breach on the injured party to determine whether the breach itself was of a condition or a warranty. Therefore, innominate terms are those whose classification is determined only once the effects of its breach are known. This gives the courts some flexibility in determining the appropriate remedy (**repudiation** and/or damages or damages only) that is fair to both parties.

KEY CASE

Hong Kong Fir Shipping Co Ltd v *Kawasaki Kisen Kaisha Ltd* [1962] 2 QB 26

Concerning: innominate terms

Facts

Kawasaki contracted with Hong Kong Fir Shipping to charter a vessel for a period of two years. A term in the contract required that the vessel was 'fitted in every way for ordinary cargo service' and that the owners would 'maintain her in a thoroughly efficient state . . . during service'. Soon after beginning the voyage the ship broke down due to the incompetence of its engine room staff and, in any event, it was discovered that it was not seaworthy and in need of many repairs.

As a result, the claimants were deprived of the use of the ship for 18 weeks while it was repaired to a seaworthy state. Kawasaki wrote to the owners repudiating the charter. Hong Kong Fir brought an action for wrongful repudiation, claiming that the term was only a warranty and not a condition.

Legal principle

It was held that Hong Kong Fir was in breach of the contract to deliver a seaworthy vessel, and also that it failed to maintain the vessel in an efficient state. However, this breach was not substantial enough to entitle the charterer to repudiation of the contract.

Lord Diplock stated that:

> There are . . . many contractual undertakings of a more complex character which cannot be categorised as being 'conditions' or 'warranties' . . . Of such undertakings all that can be predicated is that some breaches will and others will not give rise to an event which will deprive the party not in default of substantially the whole benefit which it was intended that he should obtain from the contract; and the legal consequences of a breach of such an undertaking, unless provided for expressly in the contract, depend upon the nature of the event to which the breach gives rise and do not follow automatically from a prior classification of the undertaking as a 'condition' or a 'warranty'.

Despite the fact that the use of innominate terms can leave a contractual relationship on a footing of some uncertainty, the approach taken in *Hong Kong Fir Shipping* has also been applied in later cases (*Cehave NV* v *Bremer Handelsgesellschaft mbH (The Hansa Nord)* [1976] QB 44). However, notwithstanding the introduction of innominate terms, the court will still classify a term as a condition (irrespective of the consequences of the breach) if it considers that the circumstances merit doing so (*Bunge Corporation* v *Tradax Export SA* [1981] 1 WLR 711).

■ Implied terms

As well as express terms which are part of the contract, certain terms can be implied into contracts in three ways:

- by the court
- by custom
- by statute (see Figure 4.3).

Figure 4.3

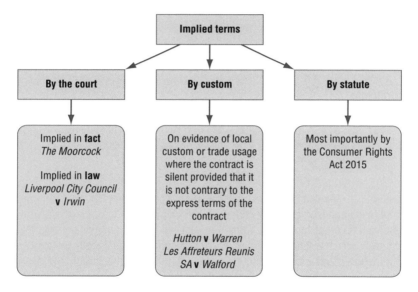

Terms implied by the court

The court may imply terms in *fact* or in *law*.

Terms implied in fact

A term will be implied in fact if it is obvious and necessary in order to give the contract business efficacy. The test used by the courts in this case is known as the officious bystander test, which was stated by MacKinnon LJ in *Shirlaw* v *Southern Foundries Ltd* [1940] AC 701, who considered that:

Prima facie that which is left to be implied is something so obvious that it goes without saying; so that, if, while the parties were making their bargain, an officious bystander were to suggest some express provision for it in the agreement, they would testily suppress him with a common 'Oh, of course!'

KEY CASE

The Moorcock (1889) 14 PD 64

Concerning: terms implied in fact

Facts

The claimant entered into a contract with the defendants to dock and unload cargo from his ship at their wharf on the Thames. The ship was grounded at the jetty at low tide and broke up on rocks. The claimant sued for the damage to his ship. The defendants claimed that there was no express term relating to the safety of the ship and, as such, they could not be liable for breach of contract.

Legal principle

The court held that there was an implied term in the contract that the ship would not be damaged. This term was necessary in order to give the contract business efficacy. Therefore the defendants were liable for breach of this implied term.

However, it does not always follow that terms will be implied in fact where they appear to be missing. In *Attorney General of Belize* v *Belize Telecom* [2009] UKPC 10, Lord Hoffmann commented that it may be that the missing term was deliberately omitted, and if the process of construction revealed that was so, then the courts should accept that the clause is not implied in fact and allow the loss to lie where it falls.

Terms implied in law

As well as terms that are implied by the courts in fact, there are terms that are implied by the courts in law. The distinction between the two is as follows:

- Terms implied in fact are inserted to represent the obvious, but unexpressed, wishes of the parties to the particular contract in question.
- Terms implied in law are inserted into the contract *regardless* of the wishes of the parties: typically to regulate a particular sort of agreement and often to protect the interests of the weaker party.

KEY CASE

Liverpool City Council v *Irwin* [1976] 2 WLR 562

Concerning: terms implied in law

Facts

The condition of a council tower block deteriorated such that the stairs and lifts were in disrepair and internal rubbish chutes were blocked. Irwin alleged a breach on the part of the council of its implied covenant for their quiet enjoyment of the property.

Legal principle

The House of Lords held that it was an implied term of the lease that the landlord should take reasonable care to keep the common parts of the block in a reasonable state of repair. The term was clearly not implied in fact. The 'officious bystander' test was not satisfied. The implication was also not required to give business efficacy to the contract.

The implication arose because the relationship between the parties made it desirable to place an obligation on the landlord as to the maintenance of the common parts of the premises. This was done by the imposition of a legal duty even though no contractual term could be implied in fact.

Customary implied terms

Terms may also be implied into a contract by custom: that is in response to (parol) evidence of local custom or usage in matters which relate to the contract in question where the contract itself is silent on the matter (*Hutton* v *Warren*). However, terms will not be implied by custom where they would be contrary to the express terms of the contract (and thus the express intention of the parties not to abide by local custom or usage) (*Les Affrêteurs Réunis SA* v *Walford*).

Statutory implied terms

Finally, certain terms are implied into contracts by statute, primarily to protect parties where there is inequality of bargaining strength. For example, there are various terms that are implied into contracts of employment. However, perhaps the most commonly encountered statutory implied terms are those relating to consumer contracts which – from 1 October 2015 – are inserted by the Consumer Rights Act 2015. Prior to this, the relevant analogous legislation was the Sale of Goods Act 1979 (as amended by the Sale and Supply of Goods Act 1994) and the Supply of Goods and Services Act 1982.

Section 3 of the Consumer Rights Act 2015 sets out the contracts that are covered by the legislation. These are contracts in which a trader supplies goods to a customer for sale, hire, hire-purchase or transfer.

The main provisions of the Act that apply to every contract to supply goods are as follows:

Consumer Rights Act 2015	Effect
Section 9(1) – Quality	Every contract to supply goods has an implied term that the quality of the goods is satisfactory
Section 9(2) – Satisfactory quality	Goods are of satisfactory quality if they *meet the standard that a reasonable person would regard as satisfactory* taking account of any description, the price and all other relevant circumstances (*Egan* v *Motor Services Bath* [2007] EWCA Civ 1002 considered this in the context of s 14(2A) of the Sale of Goods Act 1979 which used the same wording)
Section 9(3) – Quality	The quality of goods includes their state and condition and includes: ■ fitness for all the purposes for which goods of the kind in question are commonly supplied ■ appearance and finish ■ freedom from minor defects ■ safety ■ durability (This is not an exhaustive list – the statute explicitly says 'among others')
Section 9(4) – Circumstances in which quality of goods is not unsatisfactory	The quality of goods is not unsatisfactory in respect of specific defects which are specifically drawn to the buyer's attention before the contract is made; upon examination of the goods by the buyer before the contract, defects which that examination ought to reveal; or in the case of a contract to supply goods by sample, which would have been apparent on a reasonable examination of the sample ▶

Consumer Rights Act 2015	Effect
Section 10 – Fitness for purpose	In a contract to supply goods, if the buyer expressly or by implication makes known to the seller any particular purpose for which the consumer is contracting for the goods *before the contract is made,* there is an implied term that the goods are reasonably fit for that purpose (whether or not that is a purpose for which such goods are commonly supplied) *except* where the consumer does not rely, or it is unreasonable for him to rely, on the skill or judgement of the seller
Section 11 – Sale by description	Every contract to supply goods by description is to be treated as including a term that the goods will match the description

Breaches of any of these statutory terms is dealt with under section 19 of the Consumer Rights Act 2015. The consumer's remedies are:

- the short-term right to reject the goods;
- the right to repair or replacement of the goods; and
- the right to a price reduction or the final right to reject the goods.

Any defects which are identified within six months of delivery are deemed under the Act to have existed and affected the goods at the time of delivery, unless the trader can prove otherwise or the nature of the goods is such that defects could not have been identified at the time of delivery. The consumer bears the onus of proving any defects existed at the time of delivery of the goods only if the consumer is seeking to exercise their statutory remedies after more than six months from the date of delivery of the goods.

The statutory remedies are not available to consumers where any defects or breaches of the implied terms are brought to their attention by the trader prior to conclusion of the contract or if the consumer has examined the goods before purchasing them and the goods are of a type that any defects would have been identifiable on inspection.

There are similar terms implied into contracts for consumer services under the 2015 Act:

- work (section 49) – the standard of workmanship required involves the exercise of 'reasonable care and skill';
- reasonable price (section 51);
- performance (section 52) – in the absence of express provision to the contrary, services must be performed within a reasonable time.

■ Putting it all together

Answer guidelines

See the sample question at the start of the chapter.

Approaching the question

You are asked to discuss the proposition that the contents of a contract are not always written within it – in other words that the terms of the contract are not always express terms. You should realise from reading this chapter that contractual terms can arise without being expressly recorded and this is what the essay must seek to explore. Remember also that since this is a very broad question which gives you little clue as to the specific sorts of material that you should cover, it is important to spend a few moments before you start writing your answer to gather your thoughts and to sketch out a rough outline or structure to your answer. This will help to give a reasonable flow to your answer and prevent you from rambling.

Important points to include

- You could distinguish between puffs, representations and terms, explaining that puffs and representations may not be written down, and they do not form the contents of a contract; however, oral pre-contractual statements may become terms of the contract.

- If the contract is in writing then pre-contractual statements are often treated as mere representations, although this is not always the case – courts will consider the intentions of the parties (*Evans* v *Mezario*).

- Pre-contractual statements are also incorporated if they are important to one party (*Bannerman* v *White*).

- Statements may also become terms if they are made from a position of specialist knowledge or skill (*Dick Bentley* v *Harold Smith Motors* contrasted with *Oscar Chess* v *Williams*).

- Although the parol evidence rule suggests that extrinsic evidence is inadmissible, there are a number of exceptions (particularly in relation to collateral contracts – one written, one oral: *City & Westminster Properties* v *Mudd*).

- Explain the role of implied terms and their origins (by the court, in fact and in law, by custom and by statute – with examples drawn from the Consumer Rights Act 2015).

- Finally, come to a conclusion that draws together all the points and refers back to the original statement. There are many situations in which the contents of a contract are not written within it. ▶

Make your answer stand out

- Many students would discuss only the role of implied terms in an essay such as this. Therefore, your answer will be much stronger if you also consider the ways in which oral pre-contractual statements can become terms of the contract.

- The use of cases and relevant statutory provisions is essential. Since this is a very broad question, it will most likely attract a lot of answers which are based on a superficial or 'common sense' understanding of the area (resulting from insufficient revision or choosing this question as a last resort) and which consequently contain very little (or no) legal authority. Illustrating your answer with examples will demonstrate a commendable depth of knowledge which should attract better marks.

READ TO IMPRESS

Peden, E. (2001) Policy considerations behind implication of terms in law. *Law Quarterly Review*, 117: 459.

Treitel, G.H. (1990) "Conditions" and "conditions precedent". *Law Quarterly Review*, 106: 185.

www.pearsoned.co.uk/lawexpress

 Go online to access more revision support including quizzes to test your knowledge, sample questions with answer guidelines, podcasts you can download, and more!

Exclusion of liability

5

Revision checklist

Essential points you need to know:

☐ The ways in which exclusion clauses may be incorporated into a contract

☐ The common law rules relating to the validity of exclusion clauses

☐ The statutory controls placed on the operation of exclusion clauses by the Unfair Contract Terms Act 1977 and the Unfair Terms in Consumer Contract Regulations 1999

Topic map

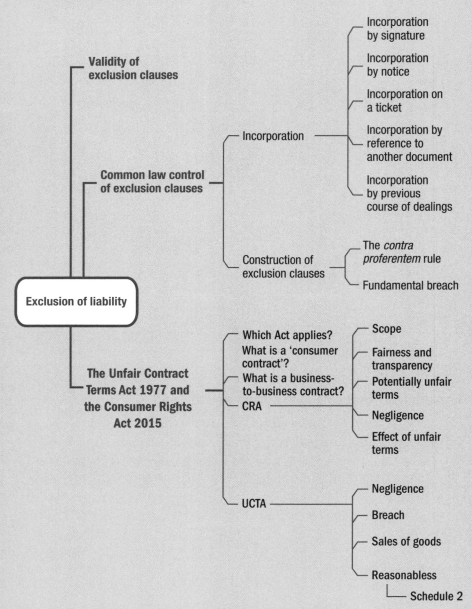

◼ Introduction

Contract terms may attempt to exclude or limit one party's liability for breach, misrepresentation or negligence.

This chapter will consider the various ways in which exclusion clauses may be incorporated into contracts. It will examine the ways in which the common law has dealt with exclusion clauses and the increasing importance of legislative intervention in their control: most importantly via the Unfair Contract Terms Act 1977 and the Consumer Rights Act 2015. These operate primarily to protect parties to contracts – particularly consumers – in situations that are considered to be 'unfair'.

ASSESSMENT ADVICE

Essay questions

Essay questions on exclusion clauses could potentially concentrate on aspects of the statutory control of exclusion clauses, the common law position, or a comparison of both. As with all essay questions, it is important to have an extensive working knowledge of all aspects of the topic. Since this is a complicated area of law, it causes confusion among students so be sure that you can outline the basic requirements for the exclusion of liability with clarity and accuracy as this will give you an excellent foundation upon which to build your analysis.

Problem questions

Problem questions on exclusion clauses very often include areas from other topics within contract law, so it would be prudent not to revise exclusion clauses in isolation.

◼ Sample question

Could you answer this question? Below is a typical problem question that could arise on this topic. Guidelines on answering the question are included at the end of the chapter, while a sample essay question and guidance on tackling it can be found on the companion website.

PROBLEM QUESTION

Mark, who runs a minicab business, agreed to sell his second-hand car to Brian for £5,000. This was a private arrangement. The sale agreement contained the following clauses:

1 This vehicle is sold as seen with no undertaking about suitability or condition.

2 The seller accepts no liability in respect of any damage, harm or injury arising from the use of the vehicle for any reason whatsoever, including, for the avoidance of doubt, negligence on the part of the seller.

Brian read the agreement before purchasing the car but did not sign it. That evening, while Brian was taking his wife Kerry out for a spin in his new car, the brakes jammed. Brian lost control and ran into a telegraph pole. As a result of the accident, Brian and Kerry were both injured. Brian suffered a whiplash injury to his back from the impact and was unable to work for six weeks. As a result, he lost £5,000 in business. An engineer discovered that the brakes had been dangerously corroded for some time and could have failed at any moment.

(a) Advise Brian.

(b) Would your answer to (a) be any different if Mark had sold the car to Brian in the course of Brian's business rather than as a private sale?

■ Validity of exclusion clauses

There are a number of means by which the operation of exclusion clauses is controlled. Historically, a body of common law developed to govern their usage and more recently statute has intervened via the Unfair Contract Terms Act 1977 and the Consumer Rights Act 2015. In order to determine whether or not a particular clause is valid, you should consider the common law position first, before applying each of the statutory controls in turn (see Figure 5.1).

✎ EXAM TIP

The Unfair Contract Terms Act 1977 is commonly referred to as 'UCTA'. We will refer to it as such in the rest of this chapter. Similarly, we will generally refer to the Consumer Rights Act 2015 as the 'CRA'. If you do the same in the exam, to save you repeatedly having to write the names of the two pieces of legislation in full each time you should make sure that you refer to them by their full name the first time you refer to them in your answer and then abbreviate them thereafter. This will prove to the examiner that you do know the full names of the relevant pieces of legislation (and their years).

Figure 5.1

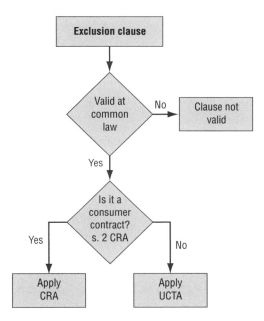

▦ Common law control of exclusion clauses

In order for an exclusion clause to be valid at common law it must satisfy three tests:

- it must be a term of the contract (that is, the clause must be incorporated in the contract);
- it must cover the damage that was caused; and
- it must be reasonable.

Incorporation of exclusion clauses

The rules of incorporation of exclusion clauses are generally the same as those which apply to the incorporation of ordinary contractual terms.

Incorporation by signature

Where a document containing contractual terms is signed, then those terms are incorporated into the contract even if the party signing did not read it or understand it. Therefore, even if a party is unaware of, or does not understand, an exclusion clause, that exclusion clause will form part of the contract if the document has been signed.

5 EXCLUSION OF LIABILITY

Note, however, that a signed contract can be invalidated in whole or in part if there is a misrepresentation as to the effect of the exclusion clause:

KEY CASE

L'Estrange v Graucob [1934] 2 KB 394

Concerning: incorporation of terms; signed contract

Facts

Mrs L'Estrange owned a café. She ordered a cigarette machine from the manufacturers which was faulty. L'Estrange claimed that Graucob were in breach of a term implied by the Sale of Goods Act 1893 that the goods were reasonably fit for their purpose. Graucob denied that the term could be implied, arguing that the contract, which L'Estrange had signed, contained a clause stating that 'any express or implied condition, statement or warranty, statutory or otherwise not stated herein is hereby excluded'. This clause was in small print and L'Estrange had not seen the clause and therefore had no knowledge of its contents.

Legal principle

The court held that the signature on the contract (order form) made the lack of awareness of the exemption clause irrelevant. When a document containing contractual terms is signed, then, in the absence of fraud or misrepresentation, the party signing it is bound and it is wholly immaterial whether he has read the document or not. The clause prevented the term from being implied and thus Graucob was not in breach, despite the faulty machine.

KEY CASE

Curtis v Chemical Cleaning and Dyeing Co Ltd [1951] 1 KB 805

Concerning: incorporation of terms; misrepresentation

Facts

The claimant took a wedding dress to be cleaned. She signed a document which contained a clause purporting to exempt the dry cleaners from liability for any damage 'howsoever caused'. When asked, the shop girl said that the clause referred only to exclusion for liability for damage to beads or sequins on the dress. The dress suffered bad staining and the claimant sued for damages. The dry cleaners attempted to rely on the exclusion clause.

Legal principle

The claim was successful. The court considered that the defendants could not rely on the exclusion clause because of the statement made by the assistant. The court said that the exclusion clause would be effective only in the event of damage to sequins or beads.

Incorporation by notice

The exclusion clause must be introduced *before* or *at the time of* the contract.

KEY CASE

Olley v *Marlborough Court Hotel* [1949] 1 KB 532

Concerning: exclusion clause; timing of notice; express notice

Facts

Mr and Mrs Olley booked into the Marlborough Court Hotel. The contract for their stay was formed at the point of check-in. While they were out for the evening, their key was taken from reception and used to gain access to their room. Mrs Olley's fur coat was stolen and she claimed damages from the hotel. The hotel attempted to disclaim liability based on a notice displayed on the wall of the Olleys' hotel room which stated that:

> The proprietors will not hold themselves liable for articles lost or stolen unless handed to the manageress for safe custody.

Legal principle

The court held that the hotel could not rely upon the exclusion clause to absolve it from liability. The contract was formed at the reception desk, at which time the Olleys had not been to their room and therefore could not have seen the notice. Hence, they were unaware of the clause at the time of the contract and, as such, it was not incorporated into the contract.

Not only must the term be introduced before or at the time of the contract, the courts require that the notice given of the exclusion clause must be *reasonable.* In other words, the party subject to the clause must be made sufficiently aware of its existence before or at the time that the contract was formed.

KEY CASE

Parker v *South Eastern Railway Co* (1877) 2 CPD 416

Concerning: incorporation of terms; reasonable notice

Facts

Mr Parker left luggage in the cloakroom at a railway station and was given a ticket in return for payment of a fee. The ticket had a clause on the back which provided that the railway company would not be liable in respect of any luggage exceeding £10 in value. ▶

Mr Parker's luggage was stolen. It was worth more than £10. The railway company attempted to exclude liability on the basis of the exclusion clause.

Legal principle

Mr Parker's claim was successful since the railway company could not prove that they had brought the claimant's attention to the exclusion clause. Therefore, since the claimant had not been made sufficiently aware of the existence of the clause he was not bound by it.

Therefore, the party who wishes to rely on an exclusion clause must take reasonable steps to bring it to the attention of the other party. However, what is reasonable is a question of objective fact. For instance in *Thompson* v *LMS Railway Co* [1930] 1 KB 41 it was noted that reasonable, *not actual,* notice is required. Therefore, an illiterate railway passenger was considered to be bound by a clause since reasonably sufficient notice had been given to the ordinary railway traveller.

Incorporation on a ticket

Parker v *South Eastern Railway* is an example of the so-called 'ticket cases' in which the courts consistently take the view that attention should be drawn to exclusion clauses by clear words.

Moreover, the clause will be incorporated only if it is on a document that might reasonably be considered to contain contractual terms.

KEY CASE

Chapelton v *Barry Urban District Council* **[1940] 1 KB 532**

Concerning: incorporation of terms; contractual document

Facts

The claimant hired two deckchairs and received two tickets from the council's beach attendant in return for payment. On the back of these tickets it was stated that 'The Council will not be liable for any accident or damage arising from the hire of the chair'. The claimant believed that the ticket was merely a receipt for payment and did not read it. One chair collapsed and the claimant was injured as a result. The claimant sued for damages; the council attempted to rely on the exclusion clause.

Legal principle

The claim was successful. The court did not accept that the exclusion clause had been incorporated into the contract since it had not been brought to the claimant's attention and held that it was unreasonable to assume that the ticket contained contractual terms.

In some instances the party seeking to rely on an exclusion clause has been required to go to great lengths to ensure that it has been brought to the attention of the other party. A very high degree of notice is required for such a clause to be effective:

KEY CASE

Thornton v *Shoe Lane Parking* **[1971] 2 QB 163**

Concerning: incorporation of terms; tickets; requirement of notice

Facts

There was a sign at the entrance to a car park which stated the parking fees and a notice that parking was 'at the owner's risk'. Drivers were required to stop at a barrier on entry to the car park and take a ticket from a machine. The barrier would then lift. Each ticket contained a statement saying that 'This ticket is issued subject to the conditions of issue as displayed on the premises'. The conditions of the contract were displayed on notices *inside* the car park. These included a clause which excluded liability for damage to property and personal injury. The claimant was injured in the car park and sued for damages. The defendants argued that they were covered by the exclusion clause.

Legal principle

The claim was successful. The court considered that the operators of the car park had not taken sufficient steps to draw the exclusion clause to the claimant's attention before the contract was made. Lord Denning concluded that the contract was formed *at the moment that the barrier was activated*:

> The customer has no chance of negotiating. He pays his money and gets a ticket. He cannot refuse it. He cannot get his money back. He may protest to the machine, even swear at it. But it will remain unmoved. He is committed beyond recall . . . The contract was concluded at that time.

Incorporation by reference to another document

Where reference is made to an exemption clause in a document given to the claimant prior to the formation of the contract, the claimant's attention must still be drawn to the clause itself.

KEY CASE

Dillon v *Baltic Shipping Co Ltd (The Mikhail Lermontov)* **[1991] 2 Lloyd's Rep 155**

Concerning: incorporation of terms; reference to another document

---

Facts

The booking form for a cruise contained a clause that the contract of carriage was 'subject to conditions and regulations printed on the tickets'. The contract of carriage was issued some time after booking at the same time as the tickets. The ship sank and the claimant was injured. The shipping company attempted to rely on the exclusion clause.

Legal principle

The claim was successful. The court held that the booking form did not do enough to draw the claimant's attention to the exclusion clause; therefore, it was not incorporated into the contract and the shipping company could not rely upon it.

This is also generally true for contracts which contain unusually burdensome contract terms. In *Interfoto Picture Library Ltd* v *Stiletto Visual Programmes Ltd* [1988] 2 WLR 615 Dillon LJ considered that:

> if one condition in a set of printed conditions is particularly onerous or unusual, the party seeking to enforce it must show that that condition was fairly brought to the attention of the other party in the most explicit way.

Incorporation by previous course of dealings

An exception to the general rule that there must be sufficient notice of the existence of an exclusion clause arises where there has been a previous course of dealing between the parties.

KEY CASE

J. Spurling Ltd v *Bradshaw* [1956] 1 WLR 561

Concerning: incorporation of terms; previous course of dealings

Facts

The parties had contracted between each other for many years for the storage of goods in a warehouse. On one particular occasion the defendant delivered eight barrels of orange juice. A few days later the defendant received a document from the claimant which acknowledged receipt of the barrels. It also contained a clause purporting to exempt the claimant from liability for loss or damage 'occasioned by the negligence, wrongful act or default' of the company and its employees or agents. When the defendant collected the barrels, some were empty and some contained dirty water. He refused to pay the storage charge. The claimant sued.

> **Legal principle**
>
> Although the document containing the exclusion clause was not received until after the contract had been formed, the court held that the clause was incorporated into the contract as a result of a regular course of dealings between the parties over the years. Since the defendant had consistently received similar documents on previous occasions without complaint or renegotiation, he was bound by the terms contained therein.

This exception to the rule will apply only if the previous course of dealings has been consistent. In *McCutcheon* v *David MacBrayne Ltd* [1964] 1 WLR 125, the claimant had sometimes been asked to sign a 'risk note' containing an exclusion clause in relation to the use of a car ferry and sometimes not. Therefore, in a claim for damages after the claimant's car was written off as a result of the ferry sinking through the defendant's negligence, the court held that the exclusion clause could *not* be relied upon since there had not been a consistent course of dealings that would have allowed them to assume that the claimant knew of the existence of the clause. As such, the clause was held not to be incorporated within the contract.

In consumer contracts, where the exclusion clause seeks to protect the (stronger) position of the seller, the courts may require evidence of a large number of past transactions in order to find incorporation via a previous course of dealings (*Hollier* v *Rambler Motors (AMC) Ltd* [1972] QB 71).

Construction of exclusion clauses

If it is established that an exclusion clause has been incorporated into the contract, it is then necessary to show that the clause covers the breach that has occurred. The contract as a whole will be considered. It is possible, therefore, that a validly incorporated exclusion clause may still fail.

The *contra proferentem* rule

The *contra proferentem* rule operates such that any ambiguity in the wording of a clause will be construed *against* the party that is attempting to rely upon it. In other words, in the event of any doubt in the wording of the clause, the benefit of that doubt will be given to the claimant.

KEY CASE

Houghton v *Trafalgar Insurance Co Ltd* [1953] 2 All ER 1409

Concerning: exclusion clause; contra proferentem *rule*

Facts

The claimant's motor insurance policy provided that the defendant insurers would not be liable if the vehicle carried an 'excess load'. The claimant had an accident while ▶

carrying six people in a five-seater car. The insurance company attempted to rely on the exclusion clause.

Legal principle

The claimant was successful. The Court of Appeal held that the term 'excess load' could mean either 'excess passengers' or 'excess weight' and interpreted it as meaning 'excess weight', using a narrow interpretation of 'load' as referring to goods and not to passengers.

If the exclusion clause attempts to exclude liability in negligence, then it must reach a very high standard of clarity and precision in drafting to be held to cover the breach that has occurred:

KEY CASE

Hollier v *Rambler Motors (AMC) Ltd* [1972] QB 71

Concerning: exclusion clause; contra proferentem *rule*

Facts

Hollier had had a service or repair done by the defendant's garage on three or four occasions. It was the defendant's practice to use a form when undertaking a repair or service, and the defendant had used its form at least twice when dealing with Hollier. When used, the form was filled in to describe the details of work to be done and the price, and signed by Hollier. The form contained a term stating that 'the company is not responsible for damage caused by fire to customer's cars on the premises'.

While Hollier's car was in the garage, it was substantially damaged by a fire that arose from faulty electric wiring on the defendant's premises which had not been properly inspected or maintained. Hollier sued the defendant for damage to the car arising from its negligence. The defendant relied on the clause set out in the invoice.

Legal principle

The claimant was successful. The Court of Appeal held that the term was not incorporated into the contract by the previous course of dealings. In any case, *obiter* the court considered that the clause did not protect the defendant. The clause was in general terms and did not refer specifically to negligence. For the garage to rely on the clause it must have stated clearly and unambiguously that it would not be liable in respect of its own negligence – otherwise a customer might reasonably conclude that the garage was not generally liable except for the situation in which the fire was caused by its own negligence.

Fundamental breach

Even where the clause does cover the breach, the courts developed a position where they tended not to allow an exclusion clause to protect a party from liability for a fundamental breach of contract. However, this doctrine of fundamental breach was ultimately rejected by the House of Lords:

KEY CASE

***Photo Production Ltd* v *Securicor Transport Ltd* [1980] AC 827**

Concerning: exclusion clause; fundamental breach

Facts

The claimants had contracted with Securicor on Securicor's standard terms to provide a night patrol to protect their factory. A clause in the standard terms provided that 'Under no circumstances shall the Company be responsible for any injurious act or default by any employee of the company unless such act or default could have been foreseen and avoided by the exercise of due diligence on the part of the Company as his employer.' One of the defendant's guards lit a fire inside the factory. This got out of control and destroyed the factory.

Legal principle

At first instance, the court held that the exclusion clause did cover the breach. On appeal, the Court of Appeal applied the doctrine of fundamental breach, reasoning that the breach was so serious that it effectively breached the whole contract and thus the exclusion clause did not apply. However, the House of Lords reversed the decision of the Court of Appeal: although the defendant company was in breach, it was allowed to rely on the exclusion clause because the clause clearly and unambiguously covered the breach that had occurred.

The Unfair Contract Terms Act 1977 and the Consumer Rights Act 2015

Although the common law had traditionally been used to control the operation of exclusion clauses, the most effective control is now found within legislation. The Unfair Contract Terms Act 1977 (UCTA) and the Consumer Rights Act 2015 (CRA) seek to impose statutory limits on the extent to which civil liability for breach of contract, negligence or other breach of duty can be avoided by means of contract terms.

Which Act applies?

As you will have seen from Figure 5.1, the first question to ask (assuming that the clause is valid at common law) is: 'Is this a consumer contract?' The answer to this question will determine which statute applies. If it is a consumer contract, the CRA will apply; if it is not a consumer contract, UCTA will apply.

What is a 'consumer contract'?

As its name suggests, the CRA deals with 'consumer contracts', that is to say, contracts between a 'consumer' and a 'trader'. Both of these terms are set out in the CRA:

- **Consumer:** an individual acting for purposes which are wholly or mainly outside that individual's trade, business, craft or profession (s 2(3)).
- **Trader:** a person acting for purposes relating to that person's trade, business, craft or profession, whether acting personally or through another person acting in the trader's name or on the trader's behalf (s 2(2)).

Note that there is an exception for employment or apprenticeship contracts which specifically are excluded from CRA protection by section 61. You should consider the parties to the contract carefully and decide, on the basis of the definitions in section 2(3), whether you have a consumer contract or not.

What is a business-to-business contract?

The operation of the CRA leaves UCTA to deal with exclusion clauses in **business-to-business contracts** only.

These are defined in section 1(3) UCTA as arising:

(a) from things done or to be done by a person in the course of a business (whether his own business or another's); or

(b) from the occupation of premises used for business purposes of the occupier.

UCTA does not extend to certain kinds of contracts. These are listed in Schedule 1 and include:

- any contract of insurance;
- any contract relating to the creation, transfer or termination of an interest in land;
- any contract so far as it relates to the creation, transfer or termination of a right or interest in any patent, trade mark, copyright or design right, registered design, technical or commercial information or other intellectual property.

CRA—scope

The unfair terms regime of the CRA is set out in Part 2 of the Act. The scope of Part 2 is provided by section 61 which specifically includes certain 'notices' as well as terms insofar as such notices relate to rights or obligations as between a trader and a consumer or purport to exclude or restrict a trader's liability to a consumer.

CRA — contract terms and notices must be fair and transparent

Section 62 of the CRA provides the general principle that contract terms and notices must be fair and if they are not, then they are not binding on the consumer (unless the consumer chooses to rely on that term or notice). Contractual terms and notices must also be transparent (section 68) – that is, plain, intelligible and legible – and in the event of ambiguity, terms and notices are given the meaning that is most favourable to the consumer (section 69).

Unfair terms are defined in section 62(4) of the Act:

KEY STATUTE

Consumer Rights Act 2015, section 62

(1) An unfair term of a consumer contract is not binding on the consumer.

(2) An unfair consumer notice is not binding on the consumer.

(3) This does not prevent the consumer from relying on the term or notice if the consumer chooses to do so.

(4) A term is unfair if, contrary to the requirement of good faith, it causes a significant imbalance in the parties' rights and obligations under the contract to the detriment of the consumer.

(5) Whether a term is fair is to be determined –

    (a) taking into account the nature of the subject matter of the contract, and

    (b) by reference to all the circumstances existing when the term was agreed and to all of the other terms of the contract or of any other contract on which it depends.

(6) A notice is unfair if, contrary to the requirement of good faith, it causes a significant imbalance in the parties' rights and obligations to the detriment of the consumer.

(7) Whether a notice is fair is to be determined –

    (a) taking into account the nature of the subject matter of the notice, and

    (b) by reference to all the circumstances existing when the rights or obligations to which it relates arose and to the terms of any contract on which it depends.

However, section 64 of the CRA goes on to elaborate on terms that are excluded from an assessment of fairness: these are terms that specify the main subject matter of the contract or the appropriateness of the price paid provided that they are transparent and prominent.

A term is prominent if it is brought to the consumer's attention in such a way that an average consumer would be aware of the term.

CRA—potentially unfair terms

Schedule 2 of the CRA sets out an 'indicative and non-exhaustive' list of 20 terms in consumer contracts that *may* be regarded as unfair. These include:

- a term that has the object or effect of excluding or limiting the trader's liability in the event of the death of or personal injury to the consumer resulting from an act or omission of the trader;
- a term that has the object or effect of requiring that, where the consumer decides not to conclude or perform the contract, the consumer must pay the trader a disproportionately high sum in compensation or for services that have not been supplied;
- a term that has the object or effect of irrevocably binding the consumer to terms with which the consumer has had no real opportunity of becoming acquainted before the conclusion of the contract;
- a term that has the object or effect of permitting a trader to increase the price of goods, digital content or services without giving the consumer the right to cancel the contract if the final price is too high in relation to the price agreed when the contract was concluded.

CRA—negligence

Section 65(1) of the CRA provides that a 'trader cannot by a term of a consumer contract or by a consumer notice exclude or restrict liability for death or personal injury resulting from negligence'. This blanket position is qualified by section 66, which excludes certain types of contract, including insurance contracts or contracts relating to land.

CRA—effect of unfair terms

Section 67 provides that where a contractual term is not binding as a result of unfairness, the rest of the contract continues to have effect so far as is practicable. In other words, the rights and obligations created by the contract continue as if the offending unfair term was simply not there.

UCTA—negligence

Section 2(1) UCTA provides that liability for death or personal injury resulting from negligence cannot be excluded by reference to any contract term or notice. Section 2(2) UCTA provides that for loss or damage other than death or personal injury, liability may be excluded or limited so far as the term satisfies the reasonableness test (see below).

UCTA—breach

Section 3 UCTA provides that where one party deals on the other's written standard terms of business, then the other party cannot exclude or restrict liability for breach of contract, unless the term satisfies the reasonableness test (see below).

UCTA—sale of goods

With the exception of consumer contracts, which are dealt with by the CRA, sections 6 and 7 UCTA deal with attempts to exclude or restrict certain terms into sale of goods, hire purchase and other contracts in which possession or ownership of goods passes. As before, these terms are subject to the reasonableness requirement.

UCTA—reasonableness

The test for reasonableness in UCTA is found in section 11.

KEY STATUTE

Unfair Contract Terms Act 1977, section 11

(1) In relation to a contract term, the requirement of reasonableness . . . is that the term shall have been a fair and reasonable one to be included having regard to the circumstances which were, or ought reasonably to have been, known to or in the contemplation of the parties when the contract was made.

(2) In determining for the purposes of section 6 or 7 [UCTA] above whether a contract term satisfies the requirement of reasonableness, regard shall be had in particular to the matters specified in Schedule 2 to this Act . . .

(3) In relation to a notice (not . . . having contractual effect), the requirement of reasonableness under this Act is that it should be fair and reasonable to allow reliance on it, having regard to all the circumstances obtaining when the liability arose or (but for the notice) would have arisen.

(4) Where by reference to a contract term or notice a person seeks to restrict liability to a specified sum of money, and the question arises . . . whether the term or notice satisfies the requirement of reasonableness, regard shall be had in particular . . . to –

    (a) the resources which he could expect to be available to him for the purpose of meeting the liability should it arise; and

    (b) how far it was open to him to cover himself by insurance.

(5) It is for those claiming that a contract term or notice satisfies the requirement of reasonableness to show that it does.

Make your answer stand out

Section 11(1) provides when the reasonableness test is to be applied – the key point here is that it must have been reasonable in all the circumstances when the contract was made. In the case of clauses that attempt to limit liability, then by section 11(4) the court must consider the resources that the defendant has available to meet that liability and whether the defendant had the possibility to protect himself by insurance. Section 11(5) establishes that the burden of proof to establish reasonableness of a contract term is on the defendant – in other words, the party that is attempting to rely upon the exclusion clause has to prove that it is reasonable within the meaning of section 11(1) (*Warren* v *Truprint Ltd* [1986] BTLC 344). It is important that you are able to demonstrate the fine differences between these points to ensure that you apply the law precisely.

UCTA, Schedule 2

Section 11(2), UCTA refers to Schedule 2 to the Act, which provides guidelines of the application of the reasonableness test. The criteria that should be considered are as follows:

- the strength of the bargaining positions of the parties relative to each other;

- whether the customer received an inducement to agree to the term (*R.W. Green Ltd* v *Cade Bros Farms* [1978] Lloyd's Rep 602);

- whether the customer knew or ought reasonably to have known of the existence and the extent of the term (having regard, among other things, to any trade custom and any previous course of dealing between the parties);

- where the term excludes or restricts any relevant liability if some condition was not complied with, whether it was reasonable at the time of the contract to expect that compliance with that condition would be practicable;

- whether the goods were manufactured, processed or adapted to the special order of the customer.

Examples of the application of the reasonableness test can be found in *George Mitchell (Chesterhall) Ltd* v *Finney Lock Seeds* [1983] 2 AC 803, *Smith* v *Eric S. Bush* [1990] 1 AC 381 and *Watford Electronics Ltd* v *Sanderson CFL Ltd* [2001] 1 All ER (Comm) 696.

Where contracts between businesses are concerned, even standard form terms are rarely regarded as unreasonable: *Röhlig (UK) Ltd* v *Rock Unique Ltd* [2011] EWCA Civ 18.

■ Putting it all together

Answer guidelines

See the sample question at the start of the chapter.

Approaching the question

This is a typical problem question that could arise on the exclusion of liability. It is important with any such question that you first spend some time acquainting yourself with the facts before working out a clear and structured approach to the question involving identification of the legal issue, the relevant law, applying the law to the facts and reaching a conclusion. Remember that you should consider both the common law position as well as the relevant statutes that apply in this area. Always look at the common law first.

Important points to include

- For Brian to be successful, he must establish that the exclusion clauses are not valid.
- **In part (a),** the key point is that the transaction is a private sale.
- Does the fact that the car had defective brakes constitute breach of contract? Since the car is not sold in the course of a business (the contract is between two private individuals), the terms relating to quality and fitness for purpose implied by section 14 of the Sale of Goods Act 1979 and section 10 of the Consumer Rights Act 2015 do not apply.
- Are the exclusion clauses incorporated into the contract? They are contained in a written sales agreement at the time of sale – so yes (*Olley* v *Marlborough Court Hotel*).
- The fact that Brian did not sign the agreement is irrelevant (*L'Estrange* v *Graucob*).
- Do the clauses cover the defect and damage? Yes – the clauses refer to no undertaking about condition and no liability for harm or injury.
- Even though this is a fundamental breach, an exclusion clause may still cover such a breach at common law (*Photo Production Ltd* v *Securicor*).
- The clauses are valid at common law.
- Private transactions are not covered by UCTA or the CRA.
- *Therefore the clauses are valid and Brian has no claim against Mark.*
- **In part (b)** the transaction is carried out in the course of a business between a trader and a consumer. This will bring the CRA into consideration, even though the clauses would most likely survive the common law tests (as shown in part (a)). ▶

- Sections 9 and 10 of CRA imply contractual terms that the goods must be of satisfactory condition and fit for purpose – it is unlikely that the car was fit for purpose at the time of sale (consider short space of time between purchase and failure and the findings of the engineer's report).

- Clause 4 will be considered in the light of the fairness tests in section 62 CRA. It will most likely fail due to being unfairly broad (and thus creating a significant imbalance in the rights to the detriment of Brian, the consumer).

- Section 65 of CRA provides that a trader cannot exclude or restrict liability in a consumer contract for death or personal injury resulting from negligence. Therefore clause 10 in the agreement will automatically fail.

- *Brian is therefore likely to be successful and will be awarded damages (compensation).*

 Make your answer stand out

- As well as stating the relevant law in relation to the contractual terms, you are being asked to advise one of the parties. You should therefore remember to cover points such as who will have the burden of proof where points are arguable.

- You should give an assessment as to the likely outcome of each claim – in terms of strength of case and remedy sought.

- Be precise when considering the many statutory provisions that apply to this area – provide pinpoint references to the statutory provisions that you are discussing.

- Avoid a confused answer by dealing with each clause separately.

READ TO IMPRESS

Adams, J. and Brownsword, R. (1988) The Unfair Contract Terms Act: a decade of discretion. *Law Quarterly Review,* 104: 94.

Bright, S. (2000) Winning the battle against unfair contract terms. *Legal Studies,* 20: 331.

Macdonald, E. (1992) Exclusion clauses: the ambit of s 13(1) of the Unfair Contract Terms Act 1977. *Legal Studies,* 12: 277.

Macdonald, E. (1999) The emperor's old clauses: unincorporated clauses, misleading terms and the unfair terms in consumer contracts regulations. *Cambridge Law Journal,* 58: 413.

Macdonald, E. (2004) Unifying unfair terms legislation. *Modern Law Review,* 67: 69.

www.pearsoned.co.uk/lawexpress

Go online to access more revision support including quizzes to test your knowledge, sample questions with answer guidelines, podcasts you can download, and more!

.

Misrepresentation, mistake and illegality

Revision checklist

Essential points you should know:

- [ ] The elements of misrepresentation
- [ ] The differences between fraudulent, negligent and innocent misrepresentation
- [ ] Remedies that may be available for misrepresentation
- [ ] The operation of common, mutual and unilateral mistake
- [ ] Remedies that may be available for mistake
- [ ] The principles of illegality in contract

◼ Topic map

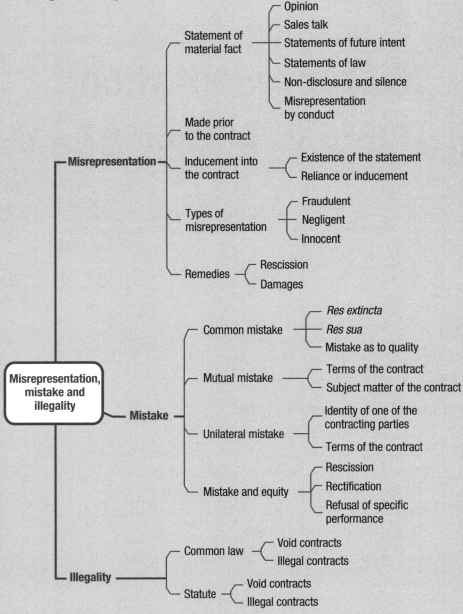

■ Introduction

Misrepresentation, mistake and illegality are factors which invalidate otherwise valid contracts.

They are also known as 'vitiating factors'. Even though a contract may be formed perfectly validly in law (that is, the elements of a binding contract – offer, acceptance, consideration and intention to create legal relations are all present), the contract may still be unenforceable due to other factors. These factors are the sorts of things that, had they been known by both parties at the time of the contract being formed, the parties might never have reached agreement and thus the contract might never have been formed. Depending on the particular circumstances, a contract may be **void** (treated as though it had never been valid at all) or **voidable** (avoided by one party; that is, it is not automatically void, but one of the parties may choose to treat it as void and thus unenforceable, or continue with it if they so desire, or amend its terms to those which are more preferable).

ASSESSMENT ADVICE

Issues covered in this chapter could arise as an essay question or form part of a problem question.

Essay questions

Essay questions on mistake, misrepresentation and illegality are common and varied. There is a wealth of case law on these topics so they can make quite difficult revision topics. Try to ensure that you have a foundation of knowledge based upon the cases that establish the key principles and then build upon this with looking at cases that demonstrate the operation of the law. Remember that an essay requires that you demonstrate an ability to engage in critical analysis so make a note of any weaknesses in the law or differences of opinions between the courts and be ready to incorporate these into your essay.

Problem questions

Problem questions involving mistake and/or misrepresentation are also common. Look out for facts that suggest that one party harboured an inaccurate belief about some fact associated with the performance of the contract as a clue that these topics are relevant. You should then consider whether this inaccurate belief was a result of some factor associated solely with the mistaken party (mistake) or whether it was planted in the mistaken party's mind by the other party (misrepresentation).

■ Sample question

Could you answer this question? Below is a typical problem question that could arise on this topic. Guidelines on answering the question are included at the end of the chapter, while a sample essay question and guidance on tackling it can be found on the companion website.

PROBLEM QUESTION

Rebecca owned a film studio. She negotiated with Thomas who owned a cinema regarding purchase of the rights to show a film for four weeks at £25,000. Rebecca said that the film was a real bargain and an extraordinary new visual experience since the film was the only one on the market to use 3D-HD photography; she also thought that the film could be shown on small screens as well as panoramic ones, although she had never shown it on small screens herself. She pointed to a report on her desk containing the estimated average takings of the film when shown at the Odeon in Leicester Square. Thomas read the report. It stated that on average the film had made approximately £75,000 a week. He thought he might send his accountant around to look at the accounts to verify the report, but decided not to. He was impressed with what Rebecca had said and, in any event, he wanted to be the first cinema in his town to show a 3D-HD film.

Thomas purchased the film. It turned out to be a disaster. The photography was ordinary. After the negotiations, but before the sale, three other films were released in London that had 3D-HD photography but Rebecca forgot to tell Thomas before Thomas bought the film. The film was not able to be shown on small screens. Thomas made only £7,000 per week over the four-week period. This was not surprising as the report had been prepared by Rebecca's trainee accountant Chris, who had got the figures wrong as he was having problems with his new laptop.

Had the mistake not been made, the report would have read £7,500 per week. Rebecca had not seen the film nor read the report before directing Thomas's attention to it. Chris has now left Rebecca's employment.

Advise Thomas whether he might have any remedy in contract against Rebecca.

■ Misrepresentation

Before considering the elements of misrepresentation in detail, it is first necessary to define what is meant by an **actionable misrepresentation**.

KEY DEFINITION: Actionable misrepresentation

An actionable misrepresentation is a statement of material fact made prior to the contract by one party to the contract to the other which is false or misleading and which induced the other party to enter into the contract.

You can see that there are a number of elements to a misrepresentation, which we will now explore in more detail.

A statement of material fact

There are certain statements that might not be treated as being statements of material fact:

- opinion
- mere sales talk
- statements of future intention or conduct
- statements of law.

It is also necessary to consider whether silence (or failure to disclose certain information) can ever amount to a misrepresentation.

Opinion

A false statement of opinion is not a misrepresentation as to fact.

KEY CASE

Bissett v *Wilkinson* [1927] AC 177

Concerning: misrepresentation; statement of opinion

Facts

The claimant purchased two pieces of land from the defendant for the purpose of sheep farming. During negotiations the defendant said that he believed that it would be suitable for 2,000 sheep. The claimant therefore bought the land in that belief. Both parties knew that the defendant had not carried on sheep farming on the land. The land would not, in fact, hold 2,000 sheep.

Legal principle

The court upheld the decision of the trial judge who considered that:

In ordinary circumstances, any statement made by an owner who has been occupying his own farm as to its carrying capacity would be regarded as a statement of fact . . . ▶

> This, however, is not such a case . . . In these circumstances . . . the defendants were not justified in regarding anything said by the plaintiff [now claimant] as to the carrying capacity as being anything more than an expression of his opinion on the subject.
>
> Therefore, a statement of opinion cannot give rise to an actionable misrepresentation. In the absence of fraud, the claimant had no basis on which to rescind the contract.

However, where the party making the statement has some special knowledge or skill that gives weight to their opinion, then their opinion may be treated as being an implied representation of fact, and therefore capable of being a misrepresentation (*Smith* v *Land and House Property Corp* (1884) 28 Ch D 7).

Sales talk

Mere 'sales talk' or 'puff' is not considered to be a statement of fact. The courts treat such utterances as idle boasts and attach no contractual significance to them.

KEY CASE

Dimmock v *Hallett* (1866) 2 Ch App 21

Concerning: misrepresentation; sales talk

Facts

During negotiations for the sale of land, the land was described as 'fertile and improvable'.

Legal principle

The court considered that this statement had insufficient substance to be classed as a representation.

This was also considered in *Carlill* v *Carbolic Smoke Ball Co Ltd* (see Chapter 1).

Statements of future intent

Since a misrepresentation is a false representation of material fact, it follows that since a statement which expresses a future intention is speculation rather than fact, it cannot amount to a misrepresentation. However, in much the same way that an opinion can be treated as fact where the party has special knowledge, if the statement of future intention falsely represents the actual intention (in other words, it is a wilful lie) then it may also be treated as a misrepresentation of fact:

KEY CASE

Edgington v *Fitzmaurice* (1885) 29 Ch D 459

Concerning: misrepresentation; statements of future intention

Facts

The claimant was a shareholder who received a circular issued by the directors of a company requesting loans to the amount of £25,000 with interest in order to grow their business. However, the money was in fact to be used to pay off the company's debt, not to grow the business. The claimant, who had taken debentures, claimed repayment of his money on the ground that it had been obtained from him by misrepresentation.

Legal principle

The court held that the untrue statement as to future intention was a misrepresentation of fact.

Statements of law

Traditionally, a false statement of law cannot amount to a misrepresentation because there is a presumption that everyone knows the law and therefore it cannot be falsely stated. However, since the distinction between fact and law is not always clear cut, it can be difficult to distinguish between a statement of law and a statement of fact:

KEY CASE

Solle v *Butcher* [1950] 1 KB 671

Concerning: statements of law

Facts

Before the Second World War, a house had been converted into flats. After the war, the defendant leased the building with the intention to repair bomb damage and undertake other improvements. The claimant and defendant discussed the rents to be charged after the work had been completed. The defendant stated that the flat had become a new and separate dwelling by reason of change of identity, and was therefore not subject to the Rent Restriction Acts.

Legal principle

This was held to be a statement of fact and therefore actionable.

However, following *Pankhania* v *London Borough of Hackney* [2002] NPC 123, it seems that a misrepresentation of law can amount to an actionable misrepresentation. Here, the particulars of a commercial property for sale by auction described it as being sold subject to a 'licence' which was terminable on three months' notice. The court held that this 'licence' was actually a tenancy and therefore was protected under Part II of the Landlord and Tenant Act 1954. The buyer had entered into a contract to buy the property on the representation that National Car Parks Ltd had a licence that was terminable on three months' notice, and was successful in his claim for damages as a result of misrepresentation. The court held that there had been a misrepresentation as to the legal character of the 'licence'.

Non-disclosure of information and silence

Generally, and perhaps unsurprisingly, silence cannot amount to a misrepresentation. In other words, there is no duty for a party who is about to enter into a contract to disclose material facts known to that party but not to the other party:

KEY CASE

Keates v ***Cadogan*** **(1851) 10 CB 591**

Concerning: misrepresentation; silence

Facts
A landlord who was letting his house did not tell the tenant that it was in a ruinous condition.

Legal principle
This failure to disclose material information was held not to be a misrepresentation.

However, this is a general rule, and the courts may decide that in particular circumstances there is a positive duty of disclosure (for example, see *Sybron Corporation* v *Rochem* [1984] Ch 112, which involved the 'covering up and deliberate concealing' of a defect).

The general rule is also subject to a number of established exceptions:

- contracts of utmost good faith (***uberrimae fidei***);
- where there has been a change in circumstances;
- half-truths;
- where there is a fiduciary relationship.

Contracts of utmost good faith (*uberrimae fidei*)
In contracts of utmost good faith there is a duty to disclose all material facts. These typically arise where one party is in a strong position to know the truth and the other is in a weak position. Examples of such contracts include the following:

- Contracts of insurance – these are the leading examples of contracts of utmost good faith. There is a duty on the insured party to disclose all material facts that are relevant to the insurer's acceptance of the risk and the insurance premium to be paid in respect of that risk. Insurance contracts are voidable if there has not been full disclosure of material facts.

■ Contracts involving family arrangements – for instance, in agreements between family members for dividing family property on death or divorce.

■ Contracts for the sale of land.

■ Contracts for the sale of shares.

Where there has been a change in circumstances

This covers the situation where the statement was true when made, but became false by the time that the contract was formed:

KEY CASE

With v *O'Flanagan* **[1936] Ch 575**

Concerning: misrepresentation; change of circumstances

Facts

During the course of negotiations for the sale of a medical practice, the vendor made representations to the purchaser that it was worth £2,000 a year. By the time the contract was signed, four months later, the value of the practice had declined to only £250 because the vendor had been ill.

Legal principle

Lord Wright MR stated that:

> . . . if a statement has been made which is true at the time, but which during the course of negotiations becomes untrue, then the person who knows that it has become untrue is under an obligation to disclose to the other the change of circumstances.

Therefore, the failure of the vendor to disclose the state of affairs to the purchaser amounted to a misrepresentation.

Half-truths

Where a statement does not represent the whole truth (in other words, if there are other facts that affect the weight of those truths stated), this may be regarded as a misrepresentation. For instance, in *Notts Patent Brick and Tile Co* v *Butler* (1886) 16 QBD 778, a purchaser of property asked the vendor's solicitor whether the land was subject to any restrictive covenants. The solicitor replied that he was not aware of any. However, while this was true, the solicitor's lack of awareness was a result of his failure to read the relevant documents (rather than having made due enquiry). This amounted to a misrepresentation.

Where there is a fiduciary relationship

A fiduciary relationship between the parties to a contract imposes a duty of disclosure. Examples of such relationships include:

- agent–principal
- solicitor–client
- partners in a partnership
- doctor–patient.

Misrepresentation by conduct

A misrepresentation can be made by conduct rather than being written or oral:

KEY CASE

Spice Girls v *Aprilia World Service BV* **(2000)** *The Times,* **5 April**

Concerning: misrepresentation; change of circumstances

Facts

Aprilia (moped manufacturers) contracted with the Spice Girls to sponsor a concert tour. The group had appeared in promotional material before Aprilia entered into the contract on 6 May 1998. This contract was based on the representation (made at the promotional photo-call) that all five members of the band, each with their distinctive image, would continue working together. Geri Halliwell ('Ginger Spice') left the band on 29 May 1998.

Legal principle

There had been misrepresentation by conduct, since the participation of all five band members in the commercial had induced Aprilia into entering the contract.

EXAM TIP

If you are considering misrepresentation by conduct in a problem question, think about what impression is given by the facts: e.g. by appearing together to promote a concert tour, the Spice Girls gave the impression that they had an ongoing working relationship when, in reality, they knew that a split was forthcoming. If the impression given is false, this may amount to misrepresentation by conduct.

Made prior to the contract

The misrepresentation must be made *before* the contract is formed. A statement that is made after formation of the contract cannot be actionable (*Roscorla* v *Thomas* (1842) 3 QB 234).

Inducement into the contract

Finally, the statement must be an inducement to the other party to enter into the contract. In other words, the claimant must have relied on, or been induced to enter the contract by, the false statement of fact. Therefore:

■ the claimant must have known of the existence of the statement; and

■ the statement must have materially affected the claimant's judgement such that the claimant was induced by it or acted in reliance upon it.

Existence of the statement

The misrepresentation must be made to the party that was misled (*Peek* v *Gurney* (1873) LR 6 HL 377) unless the claimant can establish that the party that made the statement knew that it would be passed on to them. In this case, the party making the statement can be liable in misrepresentation (*Pilmore* v *Hood* (1838) 5 Bing NC 97; *Clef Aquitaine* v *Laporte Materials (Barrow) Ltd* [2000] 3 All ER 493). It follows in either case that the claimant must be aware of the representation:

KEY CASE

***Horsefall* v *Thomas* (1862) 1 H & C 90**

Concerning: misrepresentation; claimant must be aware of the misrepresentation

Facts

The buyer of a gun did not examine it prior to purchase. A defect in the gun was concealed.

Legal principle

The court held that concealing the defect in the gun did not affect the claimant's decision to purchase as, since he was unaware of the misrepresentation, he could not have been induced into the contract by it. His claim failed.

Reliance or inducement

The claimant must actually have relied upon or acted upon the representation:

KEY CASE

Attwood v *Small* (1838) 6 Cl & F 232

Concerning: misrepresentation; reliance

Facts

The purchasers of a mine were told exaggerated statements as to its earning capacity by the vendors. The purchasers had these statements checked by their own expert agents, who erroneously reported them as being correct. Six months after the sale was complete the claimants discovered that the defendants' statement had been false. They sought to rescind the contract with the vendors on the basis of their misrepresentation.

Legal principle

There was no misrepresentation since the purchasers did not rely on the representation made by the vendor. The purchaser had relied on the verification of their agents.

It follows, therefore, that if the claimant knows that the representation is false, then there is no claim in misrepresentation, as there can be no reliance upon a known false statement.

There will be reliance even if the party to whom the representation is made is given an opportunity to verify its truth but chooses not to do so. The misrepresentation will still be considered to be an inducement (*Redgrave* v *Hurd* (1881) 20 Ch D 1).

Moreover, there will be reliance where the misrepresentation was not the only inducement for the claimant to enter into the contract (*Edgington* v *Fitzmaurice*).

Reliance may also be demonstrated by acting upon the representation:

KEY CASE

JEB Fasteners Ltd v *Marks Bloom & Co* [1981] 3 All ER 289

Concerning: misrepresentation; acting upon the representation

Facts

The defendants prepared an audited set of accounts for a manufacturing company in which the value of the company's stocks was incorrectly stated. The defendants were aware when they prepared the accounts that the company had liquidity problems and

---

was seeking outside financial support from, among others, the claimants. The claimants had reservations about the stock valuation. However, they took over the company for a nominal amount because they would thereby obtain the services of the company's two directors who had considerable experience. The takeover was not as successful as the claimants had wished and they sued the defendants for negligent misrepresentation in the audited accounts.

Legal principle

There was no misrepresentation, since the purchasers wanted to acquire the services of two of the company's directors and would have gone ahead with the purchase even if they had known the true financial state of the company.

Finally, the misrepresentation must be material. This was generally thought to mean that the misrepresentation must have been likely to affect the judgement of a reasonable man in deciding whether to enter the contract. However, in *Museprime Properties Ltd* v *Adhill Properties Ltd* [1990] 36 EG 114, the judge considered that, even where the claimant's reliance upon a representation has been unreasonable, if the representation had nonetheless induced the claimant to enter into the contract, then the representation would be held to be material.

Types of misrepresentation

Not all misrepresentations are as grave as each other. There is a sliding scale of seriousness (see Figure 6.1).

Figure 6.1

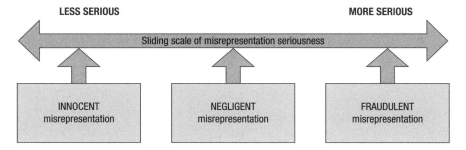

Fraudulent misrepresentation

Fraudulent misrepresentation was considered in *Derry* v *Peek*.

KEY CASE

***Derry* v *Peek* (1889) LR 14 App Cas 337**

Concerning: fraudulent misrepresentation

Facts

The defendants were directors of the Plymouth, Devonport and District Tramways Co Ltd, which was authorised by statute to run tramways by animal power, or, with the consent of the Board of Trade, by steam power. The prospectus issued by the company indicated that steam power would be used, but the Board of Trade refused its consent. The claimant, acting in reliance upon the representation in the prospectus, had obtained shares in the company.

Legal principle

This case concerned the tort of deceit. The House of Lords held that, in the absence of any evidence that the defendants believed the statement in the prospectus to be untrue, they had not committed the tort of deceit.

Lord Herschell considered the meaning of 'fraudulent' as follows:

> . . . fraud is proved when it is shown that a false representation has been made (1) knowingly, or (2) without belief in its truth, or (3) recklessly, careless whether it be true or false. Although I have treated the second and third as distinct cases, I think the third is but an instance of the second, for one who makes a statement under such circumstances can have no real belief in the truth of what he states. To prevent a false statement being fraudulent, there must, I think, always be an honest belief in its truth.

Therefore, honest belief, or lack thereof, is at the heart of fraud. Motive is irrelevant (*Akerhielm* v *De Mare* [1959] AC 789). Recklessness does not, of itself, establish fraud, unless it is a blatant disregard for the truth (and is therefore sufficiently serious to be dishonest) (*Thomas Witter Ltd* v *TBP Industries Ltd* [1996] 2 All ER 573).

Negligent misrepresentation

Historically, all misrepresentations that were not fraudulent were considered innocent and, as such, gave rise to no cause of action or remedy at common law. However, there are now actions available for certain non-fraudulent misrepresentations at both common law and statute.

Common law

At common law, damages may be recoverable for negligent misstatement that causes financial loss:

KEY CASE

Hedley Byrne & Co Ltd v *Heller & Partners Ltd* [1963] 2 All ER 575

Concerning: negligent misrepresentation

Facts

The claimant was an advertising agency which had asked the defendant bank for a reference in respect of one of its clients, which was a customer of the bank. The bank replied that the agency could assume that its client would be able to meet its financial obligations. The agency's client was in fact unable to do so.

Legal principle

The House of Lords held that negligent statements could attract liability and that this liability would extend to pure economic (financial) loss. This liability arises if:

- the defendant carelessly makes a false statement to the claimant; and
- the circumstances are such that it is reasonable to assume that the statement will be relied upon; and
- there is a 'special relationship' between the parties.

This 'special relationship' (which does not have to be contractual) between the parties gives rise to a duty of care and generally exists where the party making the statement:

- has special knowledge or skill in relation to the subject matter of the contract (*Harris* v *Wyre Forest District Council* [1988] AC 831); and
- can reasonably foresee that the other party will rely upon their statement (*Chaudry* v *Prabhakar* [1988] 3 All ER 718).

The party must, in fact, rely upon the statement, and the party which has made the statement must be aware of this (*Smith* v *Eric S. Bush*).

The principles of negligent misstatement stated *obiter* in *Hedley Byrne* v *Heller* have been applied so that it is now the case that liability arises for negligent misstatement which has induced a party to enter into a contract. This may also cover representations as to a future state of affairs.

KEY CASE

Esso Petroleum & Co Ltd v *Marden* [1976] QB 801

Concerning: negligent misrepresentation

Facts

During the negotiations for the franchise of a petrol station, a representative of Esso stated that the station would sell 200,000 gallons of fuel annually based on its proximity to a busy road. Marden contracted on the basis of this statement. The local authority then insisted that the pumps and entrance to the petrol station were moved such that the station would be accessible only from side streets and unseen by passing trade. As a result, actual sales were around 85,000 gallons. Marden lost all his money in the enterprise. Esso claimed for back rent. Marden argued that, *inter alia,* the relationship with Esso was special and created a duty of care under the *Hedley Byrne* principle.

Legal principle

The court held that the failure to disclose the change in circumstances amounted to negligent misrepresentation under the *Hedley Byrne* principle. *Per* Lord Denning:

> . . . If a man, who has or professes to have special knowledge or skill, makes a representation by virtue thereof to another . . . with the intention of inducing him to enter a contract with him, he is under a duty to use reasonable care to see that the representation is correct . . . If he negligently gives unsound advice or misleading information or expresses an erroneous opinion, and thereby induces the other side into a contract with him, he is liable [in negligent misstatement].

✎ EXAM TIP

When answering a problem question, look out for any hint in the facts that one party possesses special skill or knowledge, e.g. they may be described as being a member of a particular profession such as an accountant, or are acting in such a way that they give the impression that they have special skill and knowledge, as this is a trigger for you to consider whether negligent misrepresentation is established.

Statute

The Misrepresentation Act 1967 provides a statutory basis for a claim in respect of non-fraudulent misrepresentation:

KEY STATUTE

Misrepresentation Act 1967, section 2(1)

Where a person has entered into a contract after a misrepresentation has been made to him by another party thereto and as a result thereof he has suffered loss, then, if the person making the misrepresentation would be liable to damages in respect thereof had the misrepresentation been made fraudulently, that person shall be so liable notwithstanding that the misrepresentation was not made fraudulently, unless he proves that he had reasonable ground to believe and did believe up to the time the contract was made that the facts represented were true.

The key differences between the common law and statutory claims are illustrated in the following table:

Common law	Statute
Burden of proof on claimant	Burden of proof on defendant
No contract required	Contract required
Special relationship required	No special relationship required

Therefore, where there is a contract, and an action under the *Hedley Byrne* principle might not be straightforward, then the statutory claim under section 2(1) of the Misrepresentation Act 1967 would be preferable since it is for the defendant to prove that he had a continuing honest belief in his statement. This may be difficult to do (see e.g. *Howard Marine Dredging Co Ltd* v *A. Ogden & Sons (Excavating) Ltd* [1978] QB 574 in which the Court of Appeal – Lord Denning dissenting – held that there was insufficient evidence to sustain an argument that there was honest belief in a representation).

Innocent misrepresentation

Following the developments in *Hedley Byrne* and section 2(1) of the Misrepresentation Act 1967, it follows that an innocent misrepresentation is one that is made in the belief that it is true and that there are reasonable grounds for that belief.

Remedies for misrepresentation

The remedies that are available for misrepresentation depend on the type of misrepresentation that has occurred (see Figure 6.2).

Figure 6.2

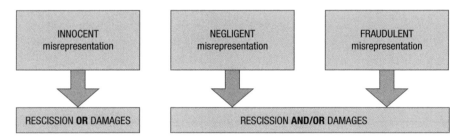

Rescission

Rescission is an equitable remedy. It involves setting the contract aside and is available regardless of the type of misrepresentation that has occurred. Rescinded contracts are terminated *ab initio*: in other words, from the very start. It follows that the object of rescission is to put the contracting parties into the position that they would have been in if the contract had never existed at all. However, there are limitations on its availability (so-called 'bars to rescission'):

- affirmation
- lapse of time
- rights of third parties
- impossible to restore parties to original positions
- damages in lieu of rescission is a better remedy.

Affirmation

Rescission will not be available if the claimant has affirmed the contract either by expressly stating that they intend to continue with it or by acting in such a way that the intention to continue with the contract can be implied from their conduct. Affirmation must be done with full knowledge of the representation and the right to rescind the contract (*Long* v *Lloyd* [1958] 1 WLR 753).

Lapse of time

Where there has been too great a lapse of time before rescission is sought, this may be evidence of affirmation and thus a bar to rescission. For fraudulent misrepresentation, the time runs from the point at which the fraud was discovered (or could have been discovered with reasonable diligence). For non-fraudulent misrepresentation, the time runs from the date of the contract itself, not the date of discovery (*Leaf* v *International Galleries* [1950] 2 KB 86).

Rights of third parties

Rescission is not available where a third party has gained bona fide rights for value in property under the contract (*Oakes* v *Turquand* [1867] LR 2 HL 325). Therefore, if goods are obtained by misrepresentation and sold in good faith to a third party, the contract cannot then be rescinded to allow the party to whom the misrepresentation was made to recover the goods from the third party (*White* v *Garden* (1851) 10 CB 919).

Restitution is impossible

Since the aim of rescission is to restore the parties to their pre-contractual position, it follows that it cannot be available as a remedy where it is impossible to do so. This may occur if the nature of the subject matter of the contract has changed (*Clarke* v *Dickson* (1858) 120 ER 463; *Vigers* v *Pike* (1842) 8 Cl & F 562). However, there is some discretion available to the court. Precise restoration is not required as long as substantial restoration is possible (*Head* v *Tattersall* (1871) LR 7 Exch 7). Diminution in value of the property is not, of itself, a bar to rescission (*Armstrong* v *Jackson* [1917] 2 KB 822).

Damages in lieu of rescission is a better remedy

Rescission may not be available if the court considers that damages in lieu of rescission provides a better remedy. This arises by virtue of section 2(2) of the Misrepresentation Act 1967:

KEY STATUTE

Misrepresentation Act 1967, section 2(2)

Where a person has entered into a contract after a misrepresentation has been made to him otherwise than fraudulently, and he would be entitled, by reason of the misrepresentation, to rescind the contract, then, if it is claimed, in any proceedings arising out of the contract, that the contract ought to be or has been rescinded, the court or arbitrator may declare the contract subsisting and award damages in lieu of rescission,

▶

> if of opinion that it would be equitable to do so, having regard to the nature of the misrepresentation and the loss that would be caused by it if the contract were upheld, as well as to the loss that rescission would cause to the other party.

The meaning of 'equitable' in this context was considered in *William Sindall plc* v *Cambridgeshire County Council* [1994] 1 WLR 1016 (CA). In this case, the claimant agreed to buy land from a local authority for development at a cost of around £5 million. After the transaction was completed, planning permission was granted for 60 houses and 30 flats on the site. However, the claimant later discovered a sewage pipe which very substantially limited the development potential of the land. The existence of the pipe had not been disclosed prior to the sale as the local authority were entirely unaware of it.

When the claimant found the sewer, the site was worth less than half of the purchase price, and the claimant purported to rescind the sale contract on grounds of misrepresentation (and common fundamental mistake – see later in this chapter).

The claimant brought an action for a declaration that the contract had been rescinded and for repayment of the purchase price with interest, which was successful at first instance. However, the appeal was allowed. On the facts, there had been no misrepresentation by the vendor. In any event, the sewer did not in practice seriously interfere with the use of the land, so that it would not be equitable for the contract to be rescinded, whether for mutual mistake or for misrepresentation and, had there been any misrepresentation, damages would have been awarded under section 2(2) of the Misrepresentation Act 1967 in lieu of rescission.

Hoffman LJ held that, if had it been necessary for the exercise of discretion under section 2(2), then the three factors for deciding what is 'equitable' would be:

- the nature of the misrepresentation
- the loss that would be caused by the misrepresentation if the contract were upheld
- the loss caused to the defendant by rescission.

Hoffmann LJ said that section 2(1) is concerned with the 'damage flowing from having entered into the contract, while section 2(2) is concerned with damage caused by the property not being what it was represented to be.'

In *Salt* v *Stratstone Specialist Ltd* [2015] EWCA Civ 745 the Court of Appeal considered whether rescission was barred by the impossibility of restitution or by lapse of time and also whether damages in lieu under section 2(2) of the Misrepresentation Act 1967 could still be awarded if rescission had become barred.

KEY CASE

Salt v *Stratstone Specialist Ltd* [2015] EWCA Civ 745

Concerning: misrepresentation; bars to rescission

Facts

A car enthusiast purchased a Cadillac car, stated to be 'brand new'. It had various defects and ultimately the claimant tried to return the car and get his money back. The defendant refused. The car was not 'brand new' – although it had not had a previous registered owner, it had already undergone a series of repairs and been in a collision, which damaged the front wheels.

In the county court, the District Judge found that rescission was barred on the basis that restitution was impossible, as the car had been registered and could not be returned as an unregistered car. He awarded damages of £3,250. The claimant appealed and the circuit judge found that rescission was not barred and ordered it. The defendant appealed to the Court of Appeal.

Legal principle

The Court of Appeal considered whether rescission was barred by the impossibility of restitution or by lapse of time and also whether damages in lieu under section 2(2) of the Misrepresentation Act 1967 could still be awarded if rescission had become barred. It emphasised that rescission was the 'normal remedy' for misrepresentation, and should be awarded if possible. It found that although the car had been registered, and the claimant had had some use of it, rescission was not barred on the basis of impossibility since registration was a legal concept that did not change the fundamental nature of the car. Rescission should be available if 'practical justice' can be done.

The Court of Appeal also considered the issue of a bar arising from delay, and *Leaf* v *International Galleries*. Roth J emphasised:

> It is something of a misnomer to say that rescission may be barred by lapse of time. It is only the lapse of a reasonable time such that it would be inequitable in all the circumstances to grant rescission which constitutes a bar to the remedy.

Finally, the courts considered whether damages would have been available under section 2(2), in lieu of rescission, had rescission been barred. It held that section 2(2) should not be seen as an additional means of claiming damages but rather as an additional restriction on the availability of rescission. The availability of damages in lieu provides a means of making the refusal of rescission fair.

Damages

Damages for misrepresentation are assessed on principles of tort law.

Fraudulent misrepresentation

For fraudulent misrepresentation, the claim arises in the tort of deceit. The intention is to return the claimant to the position that they would have been in if the misrepresentation had not been made – that is the 'out of pocket' financial loss (*McConnel* v *Wright* [1903] 1 Ch 546) as well as a possible element for 'opportunity cost' (such as the loss of profits that resulted from reliance on the misrepresentation – *East* v *Maurer* [1991] 2 All ER 733).

The claimant can recover damages for all direct loss regardless of foreseeability: in *Doyle* v *Olby* (*Ironmongers*) *Ltd* [1969] 2 QB 158 Lord Denning stated that 'the defendant is bound to make reparation for all the damage flowing from the fraudulent inducement'. This was affirmed by the House of Lords in *Smith New Court Securities Ltd* v *Scrimgeour Vickers (Asset Management) Ltd* [1997] AC 254 and applied by the Court of Appeal in *Parabola Investments Ltd* v *Browallia Cal Ltd* [2010] EWCA Civ 486.

Negligent misrepresentation

In negligent misrepresentation, a claim can be made under the principles from *Hedley Byrne* v *Heller* (provided that the tort can be established). Here (unlike in the tort of deceit) only reasonably foreseeable losses may be recovered.

Alternatively, the claimant may claim under section 2(1) of the Misrepresentation Act 1967 if there is a contract. Damages under section 2(1) are assessed on the same basis as fraudulent misrepresentation (*Royscot Trust Ltd* v *Rogerson* [1991] 2 QB 297).

Innocent misrepresentation

There is no common law action for innocent misrepresentation although rescission is still possible as an equitable remedy. If rescission is available, then damages in lieu may be available under section 2(2) of the Misrepresentation Act 1967.

 Make your answer stand out

Although it contains only three sections, the Misrepresentation Act 1967 has generated a significant volume of case law as the courts have tried to interpret its requirements. In order to obtain an insight into the difficulties posed by this Act and the way in which they have been tackled by the courts, read O'Sullivan (2001). This article provides a clear outline of the leading cases and their approach to interpretation and could give useful additional academic authority to use in the answer to an essay question.

Mistake

There is no general 'doctrine' of mistake. However, there are certain situations where a contract may be void at common law as a result of a mistake made by the contracting parties. There are three categories of mistake:

- **Common mistake:** where both parties make the same mistake.
- **Mutual mistake**: where the parties are at cross-purposes, but each believes that the other is in agreement.
- **Unilateral mistake**: where one party is mistaken and the other knows and takes advantage of the mistake.

Where a mistake is not operative, then equity may also intervene.

The effect of mistake on a contract can be depicted as shown in Figure 6.3.

Figure 6.3

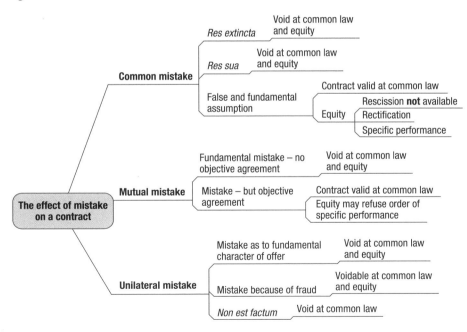

Common mistake

With common mistake there is complete agreement between the parties, but both are mistaken in regard to a fundamental point as to the existence or quality of the subject matter of the contract or the possibility of performing the contract. There are three different types of common mistake:

- *res extincta*
- *res sua*
- mistake as to quality.

Res extincta

Res extincta refers to a mistake as to the *existence* of the subject matter of the contract.

KEY CASE

Couturier v _Hastie_ (1856) 5 HL Cas 673

Concerning: common mistake; res extincta

Facts

This contract was for the sale of a cargo of Indian corn in transit. Both parties believed that the corn existed at the time of the contract. In fact, during the voyage, the cargo became overheated and fermented such that it was unfit to be carried further. The captain of the ship sold the cargo. This was customary practice. The claimant claimed on the basis that the defendant accepted the risk and should pay for the corn.

Legal principle

The court declared the contract void. Although there was no specific mention of mistake, the court considered that common sense dictated that if the subject matter of the contract did not exist at formation, then the contract did not exist either.

This proposition is now contained in section 6 of the Sale of Goods Act 1979.

KEY STATUTE

Sale of Goods Act 1979, section 6

Where there is a contract for the sale of specific goods, and the goods without the knowledge of the seller have perished at the time when the contract is made, the contract is void.

This principle may also apply where the parties contract on the basis of a mistaken assumption: in *Scott* v *Coulson* [1903] 2 Ch 249 the claimant contracted to sell to the defendant a policy of life insurance on the life of a third party. However, at the time of the contract, the third party was already dead. The contract was set aside.

However, where one party actually *warrants* the existence of the subject matter (and therefore carries the risk of its non-existence), the contract is valid. The mistake does not affect the contract: *McRae* v *Commonwealth Disposals Commission* (1951) 84 CLR 377.

Res sua

Res sua refers to a shared mistake as to the ownership of the subject matter of the contract.

KEY CASE

***Cooper* v *Phibbs* (1867) LR 2 HL 149**

Concerning: common mistake; res sua

Facts

An uncle mistakenly told his nephew that he (the uncle) was entitled to a fishery. After the uncle had died, the nephew, acting in reliance on his late uncle's statement, entered into an agreement to rent the fishery from the uncle's daughters. However, the fishery actually belonged to the nephew himself.

Legal principle

The House of Lords held that the contract was void at common law.

Mistake as to quality

A common mistake as to the *quality* of the subject matter of the contract is not sufficiently fundamental to be an operative mistake at common law. In *Leaf* v *International Galleries,* a gallery sold a painting. Both the gallery and the purchaser believed that it was by Constable. Five years later, while trying to resell the painting, the purchaser found out that it was not a Constable and therefore was worth considerably less. The court held that, in the absence of actionable misrepresentation or assumption of risk, the contract was valid.

KEY CASE

Bell v *Lever Brothers* [1932] AC 161

Concerning: common mistake; mistake as to quality

Facts

Lever Brothers entered into an agreement with one of its employees (Bell) to leave the company in exchange for £30,000 compensation. It was later revealed that there were in fact grounds for termination without compensation at the time of the agreement as Bell had previously breached his contract of employment (but had forgotten about the breaches).

Legal principle

The House of Lords held that the contract was valid since the mistake was not 'of such a fundamental character as to constitute an underlying assumption without which the parties would not have made the contract they in fact made'.

However, there are some indications that the courts may find that a contract is void for common mistake as to quality if the mistake is sufficiently fundamental: *Great Peace (Shipping) Ltd* v *Tsavliris (Salvage) International Ltd* [2002] 4 All ER 689.

✎ EXAM TIP

The important point to think about here is whether the mistake is so fundamental that a party to the contract would not have entered into an agreement if they were in possession of accurate information. Think about the facts in a problem question and put yourself in the position of the mistaken party: would you have gone ahead with the contract if you knew the reality of the situation? Although this can be a good technique to use to assess whether a mistake is fundamental, do not forget to be guided by principles derived from case law.

Mutual mistake

With mutual mistake, the contracting parties are at cross-purposes, but each believes that the other party is in agreement. They do not realise that there is a misunderstanding as to:

■ the terms of the contract; or
■ the subject matter of the contract.

Terms of the contract

The courts will try to make objective sense of the contract wherever possible.

KEY CASE

Raffles v *Wichelhaus* (1864) 2 Hurl & C 906

Concerning: mutual mistake; terms of the contract

Facts

The claimant entered into a contract to sell some bales of cotton to the defendant. The contract specified that the cotton would be arriving on the ship *Peerless* from Bombay. There were two ships named *Peerless* arriving from Bombay, one departing in October and another departing in December. The defendant, according to statements presented in court, thought the contract was for the cotton on the October ship while the claimant thought the contract was for the cotton on the December ship. When the December *Peerless* arrived, the claimant tried to deliver it. The defendant repudiated the agreement, saying that their contract was for the cotton on the October *Peerless*.

The claimant sued for breach of contract.

Legal principle

The court considered whether a reasonable third party would interpret the contract in line with the understanding of one or the other of the parties. If the court can find a common intention, the contract will be upheld. Here, the court could not determine which *Peerless* was intended in the contract. Therefore, the mutual mistake was operative, there was no agreement and the contract was void.

Subject matter of the contract

Where there is mutual misunderstanding as to the subject matter of the contract, the contract may also be void:

KEY CASE

Scriven Brothers & Co v *Hindley & Co* [1913] 3 KB 564

Concerning: mutual mistake; subject matter of the contract

Facts

The defendants bid at an auction for two lots, believing both to be hemp. In fact Lot A was hemp but Lot B was tow. Tow is considerably less valuable than hemp. Both ▶

---

lots contained the same mark, 'SL'. The purchasers had been shown bales of hemp as 'samples of the "SL" goods'. Moreover, it was unusual for different goods to be shipped under the same mark.

The defendants declined to pay for Lot B and the sellers sued.

Legal principle

The court considered that a reasonable third party could not determine whether the contract was for hemp or tow. The contract was held to be void.

However, the contract is not void where only one party is mistaken as to the quality of the goods (and performance of the contract is possible): *Smith* v *Hughes* (1871) LR 6 QB 597.

Unilateral mistake

With unilateral mistake, one party is mistaken as to the contract and the other party is aware of the mistake (or the circumstances are such that they may be taken to be aware of the mistake). This is normally a result of a mistake as to one of the following:

- identity of one of the contracting parties;
- terms of the contract;
- nature of a signed document (*non est factum*).

Identity of one of the contracting parties

If there is a unilateral mistake as to the identity of the person contracted with, the contract will be void for mistake only where:

- the identity of the contracting person is of fundamental importance to the contract (*Cundy* v *Lindsay* (1878) 3 App Cas 459); and
- this is made clear by the party who is mistaken before or at the time of the contract (*Boulton* v *Jones* (1857) 2 H & N 564).

Where a contract is made face to face, the contract is considered to be formed with the actual person irrespective of the identity assumed by that party (*Lewis* v *Averay* [1971] 3 All ER 907). This is also true where a contract is made through an intermediary (*Shogun Finance Ltd* v *Hudson* [2004] 1 All ER 215). Reasonable steps should be taken to check the identity of the other person (*Citibank NA* v *Brown Shipley & Co Ltd*; *Midland Bank plc* v *Brown Shipley & Co Ltd* [1991] 2 All ER 69).

Terms of the contract

Where there is a mistaken statement of intent by one party and the other party knows of it, then the mistake is operative and the contract is void.

KEY CASE

Hartog v *Colin & Shields* [1913] 3 KB 564

Concerning: unilateral mistake; statement of intent

Facts

The defendants were London hide merchants. They had discussed selling the claimant '30,000 hare skins at 10d (pence) per skin'. When the final offer was put in writing they mistakenly wrote '30,000 skins@ 10d per lb'. This amounted to around one-third of the price previously discussed. The claimant brought an action to hold the defendants to the written offer.

Legal principle

The court held that the claimant must have realised the defendants' error. Since this error concerned a term of the contract, the contract was void.

A unilateral mistake is operative if:

- one party is mistaken on a material term of the contract without fault (*Sybron Corporation* v *Rochem*);
- the other party knew, or should reasonably have known, of the mistake (*Wood* v *Scarth* (1858) 1 F & F 293).

Nature of a signed document—*non est factum*

Non est factum refers to a unilateral mistake concerning documents as to the *nature* of the document signed.

There must be a fundamental difference between the legal effect of the document signed and that which the contracting party thought they had signed. The mistake regarding the legal effect of the document must not result from the carelessness of the claimant (*Saunders* v *Anglia Building Society* [1970] 3 All ER 961).

Mistake and equity

If a mistake is not operative, then equity may be used in three possible ways:

- rescission
- rectification
- refusal to make order of specific performance.

Rescission

Rescission is available where it is unconscionable to allow one party to take advantage of the mistake (*Solle* v *Butcher*). However, it is not available for common mistake *(Great Peace (Shipping) Ltd* v *Tsavliris (Salvage) International Ltd)*.

Rectification

The court may rectify documents to conform to the real agreement between the parties if there is evidence that the contract does not reflect the prior agreement reached by the parties (*Joscelyne* v *Nissen* [1970] 2 QB 86). In *Chartbrook* v *Persimmon Homes* [2009] UKHL 38, the House of Lords held that it had to be demonstrated that the parties were in complete agreement but did not reflect that agreement in writing due to an error. In this case, the parties provided pre-contractual letters which showed their mutually agreed intention. However, if the mistake concerned the meaning of a particular term in the contract, then rectification will not be available (*Frederick E Rose (London) Ltd* v *William H Pim Junior & Co Ltd* [1953] 2 QB 450).

Refusal to make order of specific performance

Since equitable remedies (such as specific performance) are at the discretion of the court, the court may refuse to grant such remedies. Therefore, specific performance may be refused in the case of a mistake made by one party if:

- it would be inequitable to compel that party to perform their contractual obligations; or
- the other party knew and took advantage of that mistake (*Webster* v *Cecil* (1861) 54 ER 812); or
- the mistake resulted from misrepresentation by the other party.

However, the court will not withhold an order of specific performance to save the mistaken party from a bad bargain (*Tamplin* v *James* [1916] 2 AC 397).

◼ Illegality

Illegality is a vitiating factor that concerns itself with the character of the contract, unlike misrepresentation or mistake, which are more concerned with whether it was entered into voluntarily.

◻ REVISION NOTE

The extent to which illegality is covered as a vitiating factor varies between courses. Therefore, some courses will consider illegality in greater depth than is possible within this revision guide. You should therefore check your course syllabus carefully to see whether you need to do some further revision in this area.

Considerations of public policy are a major factor. Contracts may be void or illegal at common law or by statute:

Common law	Statute
Illegal	
In general those that are harmful on grounds of public policy as impinging upon freedom of contract, such as:	Contracts declared illegal upon formation by statute for public policy reasons (*Re Mahmood and Ispahani* [1921] 2 KB 716)
■ Contracts to commit crime or benefit from crime (*Allen* v *Rescous* (1676) 2 Lev 174)	Void *ab initio* – therefore, unenforceable
■ Contracts to defraud Inland Revenue (now HM Revenue & Customs) (*Napier* v *National Business Agency* [1951] 2 All ER 264)	Contracts formed legally but performed illegally (*Hughes* v *Asset Managers plc* [1995] 3 All ER 669)
■ Contracts concerning corruption in public life (*Parkinson* v *College of Ambulance Ltd* [1925] 2 KB 1)	Where one party is unaware of illegality, some remedies may be available, particularly where the illegality is a peripheral issue
■ Contracts to promote immorality (*Pearce* v *Brooks* (1866) LR 1 Ex 213)	
Void	
Contracts ousting the jurisdiction of the courts	Restrictive trading agreements ('solus' agreements)
Contracts undermining marriage	Competition Act 1998; Articles 101 and 102 TFEU
Contracts in restraint of trade (*Esso Petroleum Co Ltd* v *Harper's Garage (Stourport) Ltd* [1968] AC 269)	Consequences depend on wording of statute; if silent, common law rules apply
Offending clause may be removed if possible without altering the meaning of the contract, provided the outcome is not abhorrent to public policy	

■ Putting it all together

Answer guidelines

See the sample question at the start of the chapter.

Approaching the question

This is a typical problem question that raises various issues of misrepresentation. As with all problem questions, you should ensure that you have a good handle on the facts so that you can set out a structured and methodical approach to each of the legal issues that arise in turn. Remember the basic structure: identify the issues, state the law, apply the law to the facts and reach a conclusion.

Important points to include

- You could start by briefly explaining the difference between pre-contractual and contractual statements.
- Contractual statements are terms of the contract.
- Representations are pre-contractual statements: if false these are misrepresentations.
- Actionable misrepresentation must be proved.
- Define 'actionable' misrepresentation: false statement of material fact by one contracting party to the other before the contract was made which induced the claimant to enter into the contract.
- You should then consider the factual situation and decide whether any of the statements made were 'actionable' or merely statements of opinion, considering (for instance) *Dimmock* v *Hallet, Bisset* v *Wilkinson, Smith* v *Land and House Property Corp.*
- Does Thomas have a duty to verify Rebecca's statement? No (*Redgrave* v *Hurd*; *Attwood* v *Small*).
- Does it matter that the misrepresentation was not the only inducement? Consider *Edgington* v *Fitzmaurice.*
- You should distinguish between fraudulent (*Derry* v *Peek*), negligent (*Hedley Byrne* v *Heller, Esso Petroleum* v *Marden*) and innocent misrepresentation.
- Consider the remedies available at common law and statute:
  - ☐ common law: burden of proof on Thomas:

- fraudulent: damages and/or rescission, consequential damages recoverable if not too remote (*Doyle* v *Olby*; *Smith New Court Securities Ltd* v *Scrimgeour Vickers*); possible to recover for loss of profit (*East* v *Maurer*);
- negligent: damages and/or rescission (*Hedley Byrne* v *Heller*), special relationship needed (*Esso Petroleum*);
- innocent: no remedy at common law, only in equity;

☐ Misrepresentation Act 1967, section 2(1):

- negligent: burden of proof shifts onto defendant (*Howard Marine* v *Ogden*);
- damages and/or rescission; measure of damages same as for fraudulent misrepresentation (*Royscot Trust Ltd* v *Rogerson*);

☐ Misrepresentation Act 1967, section 2(2):

- negligent or wholly innocent: damages (in the form of indemnity) in lieu of rescission if rescission is barred (state the bars) or is too harsh a remedy (*William Sindall* v *Cambridgeshire County Council*).

■ Preferred action falls under Misrepresentation Act, section 2(1); damages assessed on tort basis to put Thomas into the position he was in before the contract was made.

✓ Make your answer stand out

■ There are many propositions of law to consider in answering this problem. It is important to break your answer down into as many small pieces as possible. For each proposition of law you should provide suitable case authority.

■ Ensure that you consider all the pertinent facts given to you in the question. Examiners seldom introduce facts as 'red herrings'. Your ability to apply the law to the facts effectively shows good depth of understanding and analysis.

■ You might also consider the possibility of Rebecca's statement being a term of the contract, in which case Thomas could claim for all foreseeable losses to put him into the position he would have been in had the contract been properly performed.

READ TO IMPRESS

Atiyah, P. and Treitel, G. (1967) Misrepresentation Act 1967. *Modern Law Review,* 30: 369.

Beale, H. (1995) Damages in lieu of rescission for misrepresentation. *Law Quarterly Review,* 111: 60.

Buckley, R. (2000) Illegal transactions: chaos or discretion? *Legal Studies,* 20: 155.

O'Sullivan, J. (2001) Remedies for misrepresentation: up in the air again. *Cambridge Law Journal,* 60: 231.

Slade, C. (1954) Myth of mistake in the English law of contract. *Law Quarterly Review,* 70: 385.

Smith, J.C. (1994) Contract – mistake, frustration and implied terms. *Law Quarterly Review,* 110: 400.

www.pearsoned.co.uk/lawexpress

Go online to access more revision support including quizzes to test your knowledge, sample questions with answer guidelines, podcasts you can download, and more!

Duress and undue influence

7

■ Topic map

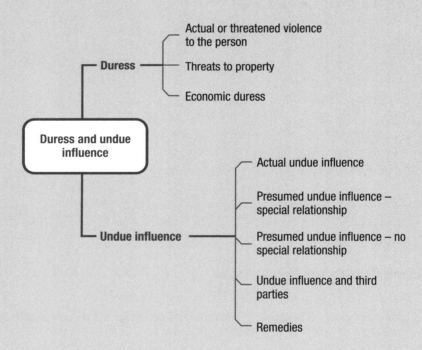

Duress
- Actual or threatened violence to the person
- Threats to property
- Economic duress

Duress and undue influence

Undue influence
- Actual undue influence
- Presumed undue influence – special relationship
- Presumed undue influence – no special relationship
- Undue influence and third parties
- Remedies

A printable version of this topic map is available from **www.pearsoned.co.uk/lawexpress**

Introduction

It is of fundamental importance that parties to a contract enter into the agreement voluntarily rather than as a result of pressure (duress) or manipulation (undue influence).

This chapter will explore the operation of the common law doctrine of duress and the equitable doctrine of undue influence. An understanding of these doctrines is important to your understanding of contract law as duress and undue influence render an otherwise valid contract voidable on the action of the wronged party, which means that the party who has been subjected to duress or undue influence can avoid being bound by the contract.

ASSESSMENT ADVICE

Issues covered in this chapter could arise as an essay question or form part of a problem question.

Essay questions

Essay questions may focus on specific issues, e.g. an evaluation of the law on economic duress, or you may encounter a more general question that asks you to discuss ways in which an otherwise binding contractual obligation may be avoided. If the latter type of question arises, remember that it is not only duress and undue influence that render the contract voidable that should be discussed but also topics such as mistake and misrepresentation.

Problem questions

Problem questions involving duress and undue influence are popular with examiners. The facts often give rise to a combination of duress and undue influence in order to test your ability to differentiate between the two doctrines. Problem questions often mingle these doctrines with misrepresentation and mistake so it might be advisable to treat these topics as a single area of revision. Look out for evidence in the facts that there has been pressure (duress) or persuasion (undue influence) by one party or the other as this should trigger a consideration of these topics.

■ Sample question

Could you answer this question? Below is a typical problem question that could arise on this topic. Guidelines on answering the question are included at the end of the chapter, while a sample essay question and guidance on tackling it can be found on the companion website.

PROBLEM QUESTION

Mrs Smith is a 72-year-old widow. She owns a freehold house, valued at £600,000. Five years ago she took in Mr Jones as a lodger. She soon came to trust Mr Jones and let him manage her financial affairs. However, Mrs Smith found out that Mr Jones had served a prison sentence for theft. Two years ago, Mr Jones persuaded Mrs Smith to transfer a one-third share in her house to him. Mrs Smith did so because she was beginning to be fearful of Mr Jones.

Six months later, Mr Jones decided that he wanted to start a new business selling double-glazing. Since he was unable to raise the necessary start-up capital on his own, he persuaded Mrs Smith to put up her remaining two-thirds share of the house as security against a bank loan in his favour. Mrs Smith signed the necessary documents at the bank in the presence of Mr Jones. Now, seven months later, Mr Jones's business venture has collapsed and he is no longer able to make payments on the loan. The bank now intends to take possession of the house.

Advise Mrs Smith whether she might be able to have any of the agreements set aside.

■ Duress

It is an essential characteristic of contract law that the parties enter into an agreement voluntarily. As such, a party who has been coerced into entering into a contract may be able to avoid the obligations of the contract by reliance upon duress, although much depends on the sort of pressure that has been applied to the claimant.

Actual or threatened violence to the person

Historically, the only sort of pressure that the courts were prepared to recognise as amounting to duress involved personal violence or threats of personal violence.

Barton v *Armstrong* [1975] 2 All ER 465

Concerning: duress and threats of violence

Facts

The claimant was the managing director of a company of which the defendant was the former chairman. The defendant threatened to kill the claimant if he did not purchase shares from the defendant. The claimant purchased the shares but sought a declaration that the transaction was void for duress. There was evidence to suggest that the claimant had been partly influenced by the threats and partly motivated by business considerations as the purchase of the shares was a good move for him and the company.

Legal principle

The court held that the contract was voidable because the threats of personal violence were a factor in the claimant's decision to purchase the shares even though he may have entered into the contract even without threats being made. In cases involving threats of violence, the onus was on the defendant to establish that these threats made no contribution to the claimant's decision to enter into a contract.

It is clear that once actual or threatened violence has been established, the claimant will be able to avoid the contract unless the defendant succeeds in the onerous task of establishing that these threats played no part whatsoever in the claimant's decision to enter into the contract. Therefore, as long as threats of violence are *a* reason that the claimant entered into the contract, duress will be established even though threats of violence were not the *only* reason.

Threats to property

For many years, the courts refused to accept that threats to damage or remove property would amount to duress. It is likely that this was because the pressure involved does not seem sufficient to amount to compulsion to enter into a contractual arrangement. For example, in *Skeate* v *Beale* (1840) 11 Ad & El 983, the claimant only paid the amount demanded as the defendant threatened to seize goods if payment was not forthcoming. Irrespective of this, the court refused to accept that this was sufficient to amount to duress.

This approach has been rejected and the courts now recognise that threats directed at property may amount to duress. This principle was stated by Kerr J in *Occidental Worldwide Investment Corporation* v *Skibs A/S Avanti (The Siboen and The Sibotre)* [1976] 1 Lloyd's Rep 293:

> If I should be compelled to sign a . . . contract for a nominal but legally sufficient consideration under an imminent threat of having my house burnt down or a valuable

picture slashed through without any threat of physical violence to anyone, I do not think that the law should uphold the agreement . . . The true question is ultimately whether or not the agreement in question is to be regarded as having been concluded voluntarily.

Economic duress

The expansion of duress to include threats to property that was stated in *The Siboen and The Sibotre* paved the way for the development of the concept of economic duress.

KEY CASE

***North Ocean Shipping Co v Hyundai Construction Co (The Atlantic Baron)* [1979] QB 705**

Concerning: duress by economic pressure

Facts

A contract existed for the construction of a boat (*The Atlantic Baron*) but the shipbuilders sought to increase the price after building had commenced due to fluctuations in the exchange rate. The purchaser did not want to agree to the variation in terms but feared that refusal would delay the completion of the boat, which would have jeopardised a lucrative charter agreement that was being negotiated on the basis of the original completion date of the boat. The purchaser paid the increased price, but eight months after delivery of the boat sought to recover the additional sum by claiming that their agreement had been obtained by duress.

Legal principle

It was held that pressure of this nature could amount to duress. The court held that the essence of duress was that there had been 'compulsion of the will' and this could arise just as much from economic pressure as it could from threats of violence. In this case, the claim was unsuccessful, not due to the nature of the pressure but due to the delay in commencing action.

Economic duress simply refers to the focus of the pressure: rather than threats being made to harm a person, the threat is directed towards their financial well-being. This does not have to be a direct 'I'll bankrupt your business if you don't sign this contract' sort of threat. Most instances of economic duress are indirect, for example: 'I will not do business with you unless you reduce your prices by half.' The essence of duress is the 'do this or else' pressure but it does not have to be expressed as a direct threat provided there is evidence of sufficient compulsion.

The principle of economic duress was accepted in subsequent cases, but there has been some elaboration on the requirements that must be satisfied.

KEY CASE

Pao On v *Lau Yiu Long* [1980] AC 614

Concerning: the requirements of economic duress

Facts

The claimants threatened not to proceed with the sale of shares unless the defendants agreed to renegotiation on other peripheral issues. The defendants wanted to avoid litigation and were anxious to reach agreement for the sale of the shares so agreed. The claimants tried to enforce the agreement but the defendants resisted on the basis of duress. The Privy Council found in favour of the claimants on the basis that the facts disclosed ordinary commercial pressure that was not sufficient to amount to duress.

Legal principle

The Privy Council stated that duress requires 'coercion of the will which vitiates consent' so that any seeming agreement was given involuntarily. Lord Scarman identified a list of factors that indicated that duress was established:

■ Did the person who claims to have been coerced protest at the time?

■ Did he have an alternative course of action open to him?

■ Did he have access to independent advice?

■ Did he take steps to avoid the contract after it was formed?

Lord Scarman identified these factors in order to ascertain whether the innocent party's agreement was involuntary. The factors themselves seem reasonable in identifying duress: we would expect a party who had been forced into an agreement to object at the time and to try to escape the obligation as soon as possible afterwards. Equally, it does not seem reasonable to categorise a situation as duress if the innocent party had other alternatives available to them as choice implies voluntary decision making. While the factors themselves cannot be criticised, later cases did take issue with Lord Scarman's assertion that duress involved an involuntary decision.

KEY CASE

Universal Tankships v *International Transport Workers Federation (The Universal Sentinel)* [1983] AC 366

Concerning: the availability of a practical alternative

Facts

A strike organised by ITWF was delaying the production of a ship that was being built for the claimant. ITWF agreed to end the strike if payments were made into its funds. ▶

The claimant made a payment but sought to recover the payment on the basis that it was obtained by duress.

Legal principle

It was held that it was not appropriate to talk about duress in terms of involuntary agreement and absence of choice as the innocent party always had a choice even if this was between two unpleasant alternatives, e.g. either pay into the union funds or lose income because the production of the boat is delayed. Lord Diplock stated that it was more appropriate to formulate a test in terms of whether the innocent party was given any practical alternative other than to comply with the other party's demands.

 Make your answer stand out

Economic duress has generated a great deal of case law and associated academic debate. It would be a valuable contribution to your revision of this topic to read articles that comment on the availability and operation of economic duress as this would help you prepare to write a well-informed essay on the topic. Chandler (1989) provides an insightful critical assessment of some of the earlier case law, while Smith (1997) provides an interesting discussion of more recent developments in this area of law.

The courts have had to decide what sort of threats will fall within economic duress. It is generally accepted that threats of unlawful action will amount to illegitimate pressure but there are situations in which threats of lawful action may amount to duress if they leave the innocent party with no reasonable alternative other than to acquiesce to the other party's demands.

Threats of unlawful action: *Atlas Express Ltd* v *Kafco* [1989] 1 All ER 641	Threats of lawful action: *CTN Cash & Carry* v *Gallagher* [1994] 4 All ER 714
Kafco was a small company that made basketware and had secured a contract to supply Woolworths. It engaged the claimant to transport the goods but, due to a miscalculation of the costs involved, the claimant increased the price of delivery after the contract had commenced and threatened to cease delivery in breach of contract if the new	The defendant supplied leading brands of cigarettes. A consignment of cigarettes ordered by the claimants went astray and the defendant agreed to re-deliver but the goods were stolen prior to delivery. A replacement consignment of cigarettes was delivered to the claimants but the defendant demanded payment for these and the stolen cigarettes. The claimants were

price was not accepted by the defendant. As failure to supply goods to its major client in the pre-Christmas period would lead to a loss of customer, the defendant felt compelled to accept the higher price but later refused to pay, claiming duress. It was held that this did amount to economic duress as the threat to breach the contract was illegitimate pressure and, due to the time frame involved, the defendant would have been unable to find an alternative means of ensuring that its goods reached the customer.

told that their credit facilities would be withdrawn if they did not agree to pay for the stolen cigarettes so they agreed but subsequently claimed that the agreement was obtained by duress. The court held that the threat of lawful action (to withdraw credit facilities) could amount to illegitimate pressure but that it did not do so in this situation. It was noted that it would require extreme circumstances before 'lawful act duress' would be recognised in a commercial contract.

Figure 7.1 illustrates the borderline between legitimate commercial pressure and economic duress.

Figure 7.1

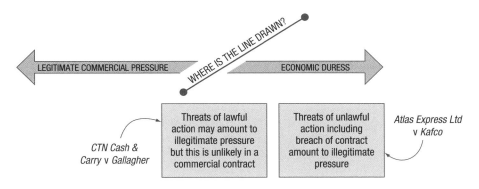

In *Progress Bulk Carriers Ltd* v *Tube City IMS LLC (The Cenk K)* [2012] EWHC 273 (Comm) the High Court commented that 'illegitimate pressure' can be constituted by conduct that is not unlawful – although it would be an unusual occurrence, particularly in the commercial context.

■ Undue influence

Undue influence is an equitable remedy (and therefore available at the court's discretion). It covers situations where one party has gained an unfair advantage over the other by applying improper pressure (which does not amount to duress at common law). The term 'undue influence' is inherently imprecise and the courts have not provided a precise definition. However, in *Bank of Credit and Commerce International* v *Aboody* [1990] 1 QB 923 the courts defined two classes of undue influence:

- class 1 – actual undue influence;
- class 2 – presumed undue influence.

The latter classification was further refined in *Barclays Bank plc* v *O'Brien* [1993] 4 All ER 417 such that the second class was subdivided as follows:

- class 2A – presumed undue influence (arising from a special relationship between the parties);
- class 2B – presumed undue influence (no special relationship in the sense of class 2A, but a relationship of trust and confidence).

Actual undue influence

For this class, there are no circumstances in which undue influence may be presumed, so the party alleging undue influence must prove the undue influence: at the time of the contract, they were not able to exercise free will in entering into it:

KEY CASE

Williams v *Bayley* (1866) LR 1 HL 200

Concerning: actual undue influence

Facts

A young man forged his father's signature on some promissory notes and presented them to a bank, which discovered the forgery. At a meeting between the bank, the father and the son, the bank threatened to prosecute the son unless some satisfactory arrangement could be reached. As a result, the father entered into an agreement to mortgage his property to pay for the notes.

Legal principle

The agreement was set aside on the grounds of undue influence since the father could not be said to have entered the agreement voluntarily.

Aboody also required the party alleging undue influence to show that they had suffered a manifest disadvantage as a result although this requirement was subsequently rejected by the House of Lords in *CIBC Mortgages* v *Pitt* [1993] 4 All ER 433.

Presumed undue influence – special relationship

Within class 2A, there is a presumption of undue influence which arises when there is a special relationship between the parties. The party alleging undue influence has to prove the existence of the relationship. The burden then falls on the other party to prove that there has been no undue influence. They must show that:

- the party alleging undue influence had full knowledge of the character and effect of the contract when entering into it; satisfied if
- the party alleging undue influence had independent and impartial advice before entering into the contract.

Special relationships

There are certain special relationships which give rise to a presumption of class 2A undue influence:

Relationship	Example
Parent–child	*Lancashire Loans Co* v *Black* [1933] 1 KB 380
Religious leader–disciple	*Allcard* v *Skinner* (1887) 36 Ch D 145
Trustee–beneficiary	*Benningfield* v *Baker* (1886) 12 App Cas 167
Doctor–patient	*Dent* v *Bennett* (1839) 4 My & Cr 269
Solicitor–client	*Wright* v *Carter* [1903] 1 Ch 27

You should note that the relationship between husband and wife was specifically excluded from the class 2A special relationship in *Midland Bank* v *Shepherd* [1988] BTLC 395.

 Make your answer stand out

You might find the exclusion of the husband and wife relationship from the class 2A special relationships surprising. This position is explored in detail by Auchmuty (2002) in her article, which provides a clear explanation of some of the leading cases and argues that the test for undue influence focuses on business relationships, thus failing to protect women who are in a vulnerable position. This may give you some useful ideas for criticisms that can be made about this topic, which could be used in an essay question.

Presumed undue influence – no special relationship

Where there is no special relationship between the parties in the class 2A sense, it is still possible for a party alleging undue influence to give rise to a presumption of undue influence if there is a relationship of trust and confidence.

It most commonly covers the relationship between husband and wife, particularly where one is induced to put up the family home as security for a loan made to the other.

It may also extend to the relationship between a bank and its client (*Lloyds Bank plc* v *Bundy* [1979] QB 326).

Finally, it may apply where the transaction itself 'calls for an explanation' (*Royal Bank of Scotland plc* v *Etridge (No. 2)* [2001] 4 All ER 449). In other words, the transaction must constitute a disadvantage sufficiently serious so that evidence is required to rebut the presumption that it was procured by undue influence.

Smith v *Cooper* [2010] EWCA Civ 722 concerned a couple who formed a relationship. Cooper, who suffered from a mental health condition, transferred a 50 per cent share in her home to Smith, who 'ran her finances'. The Court of Appeal held that, by reason of Cooper's mental condition and Smith's subsequent taking control of her finances, a presumption of undue influence arose. The same solicitor had acted for both parties and had not offered Cooper any independent advice. The presumption had not, contrary to the trial judge's finding, been rebutted, and the transaction was set aside.

Undue influence and third parties

Many cases involve putting undue influence on a party to induce them into entering into a contract with a third party: for instance, a husband persuading his wife (or vice versa) to enter into an agreement with the bank to provide security for a loan. Here, due to privity of contract, the influencer will have no contractual relationship with the third party.

However, the third party may have *constructive notice* of the undue influence.

> **□ REVISION NOTE**
>
> You may wish to refresh your memory on the doctrine of privity here. See Chapter 3.

If the transaction is one that is:

■ on its face not to the financial advantage of the party seeking to set it aside; and
■ if there is a substantial risk of its having been obtained by undue influence,

then the third party will have constructive notice of undue influence giving the right to set aside the transaction (*Barclays Bank* v *O'Brien* (1993)).

However, if the transaction is capable of benefiting the party who seeks to set it aside, the third party will *not* have constructive notice of any undue influence which may in fact have existed (*CIBC Mortgages* v *Pitt* (1993)).

The third party must then show that it took reasonable steps to ensure that the potentially influenced party entered into the transaction freely and with full knowledge of the facts.

The rules that apply where a wife claims that her consent was obtained by the undue influence of her husband were set out in *Royal Bank of Scotland plc* v *Etridge (No. 2)* (2001).

KEY CASE

***Royal Bank of Scotland plc* v *Etridge (No. 2)* [2001] 4 All ER 449**

Concerning: undue influence; third parties

Facts

A bank had taken a charge over a wife's property as security for a loan for her husband's business overdraft. The wife signed the charge in the presence of her husband. She had taken advice from a solicitor appointed by the bank, although she thought the solicitor was instructed by her husband. The bank tried to enforce the charge and the wife claimed undue influence.

Legal principle

The House of Lords considered that where a bank hopes to be protected by the fact that the wife will be advised by a solicitor it should communicate directly with the wife informing her that for her own protection it will require written confirmation from a solicitor that the solicitor has explained to her the nature of the documents and the practical implications of the transaction.

Remedies

If undue influence is successfully pleaded, then it renders the contract voidable. However, the remedy may be ineffective if the value of the property has changed.

KEY CASE

***Cheese* v *Thomas* [1994] 1 FLR 118**

Concerning: undue influence; remedies   ▶

Facts

Mr Cheese (aged 84) contributed £43,000 towards the purchase of a property costing £83,000. His nephew provided the remainder by way of mortgage. Legal title to the property was in the nephew's sole name. The property, however, was to be solely occupied by Cheese until his death. The nephew defaulted on the mortgage. The uncle claimed undue influence to secure the return of his £43,000.

Legal principle

The court accepted the plea of undue influence. They ordered the house to be sold with the uncle receiving a 43 ÷ 83 share in the proceeds. However, property prices had slumped and the house was sold for only £55,000, leaving the uncle with only around £28,500.

■ Putting it all together

Answer guidelines

See the sample question at the start of the chapter.

Approaching the question

This is a typical problem question that involves a situation in which one party to a contract may seek to rely on either duress or undue influence. It is often easy to identify that these topics are raised on the facts but far more difficult to identify where the line is drawn between duress and undue influence, so you will need to deal with these issues carefully. It is often a good idea to ask yourself whether the situation could be categorised as one involving actual pressure (duress) or heavy persuasion (undue influence). If you are in doubt, consider both options but do try to be decisive and opt for one rather than the other wherever possible to demonstrate that you understand the difference between them. As always, remember your problem solving technique: state the issue, identify the law, apply the law to the facts and reach a conclusion.

Important points to include

Deal with events as they occur so start by considering the transfer of the one-third share of the house to Mr Jones and, then, once that discussion is complete, consider the second transaction in which Mrs Smith uses her remaining two-thirds share in her house to guarantee the bank loan.

In relation to the first transaction, consider whether there is any evidence of actual or threatened physical violence (*Barton* v *Armstrong*). Mrs Smith finds out that Mr Jones has served a prison sentence but this would not suffice as the basis for duress. What is needed is for Mr Jones to have used or threatened violence. We have to ask, though, what it was that made Mrs Smith become 'fearful' of Mr Jones but, on the evidence that is available, there does not seem to be a basis upon which to rely on duress here.

The facts state that Mr Jones 'persuaded' Mrs Smith to transfer a one-third share of her house to him, which means that it is necessary to consider undue influence. Consider the three categories identified in *BCCI* v *Aboody* and *Barclays Bank* v *O'Brien*: class 1 (actual, burden of proof on claimant), class 2A (presumed, arises from a special relationship) and class 2B (presumed, no special relationship). The relationship is presumed to fall into class 2B with Mr Jones being the stronger party: *Lloyds Bank* v *Bundy*.

There is no evidence of duress in relation to the use of the two-thirds share in the house to guarantee the loan, so simply explain this and move straight to a consideration of undue influence. Mrs Smith will argue that the bank had constructive notice of the undue influence exercised by Mr Jones (*Barclays Bank* v *O'Brien*). The issue will be whether the bank was aware of the relationship.

 Make your answer stand out

Point out the difference between the common law principle of duress and the equitable nature of undue influence with a discussion of the potential bars to rescission, particularly lapse of time.

The issue regarding undue influence in relation to the use of the house as security is particularly tricky as it involves a charge over the property by a bank. Make sure that you are able to deal with this sort of situation by paying close attention to the points made in *Etridge (No. 2)* that address the position of banks and the nature and extent of the advice that they are expected to provide.

READ TO IMPRESS

Auchmuty, R. (2002) Men behaving badly: an analysis of English undue influence cases. *Social and Legal Studies,* 257.

Birks, P. (2004) Undue influence as wrongful exploitation. *Law Quarterly Review,* 120: 34.

Chandler, P.A. (1989) Economic duress: clarity or confusion? *Lloyd's Maritime and Commercial Law Quarterly,* 270.

Smith, S.A. (1997) Contracting under pressure: a theory of duress. *Cambridge Law Journal,* 56: 343.

www.pearsoned.co.uk/lawexpress

Go online to access more revision support including quizzes to test your knowledge, sample questions with answer guidelines, podcasts you can download, and more!

8 Discharge of a contract

Revision checklist

Essential points you should know:

- ☐ The rule relating to discharge by performance and its exceptions
- ☐ The ways in which a contract may be discharged by agreement between the parties
- ☐ The consequences of breach of contract and the distinction between anticipatory and repudiatory breaches
- ☐ The evolution of the doctrine of frustration and the operation of the Law Reform (Frustrated Contracts) Act 1943

Topic map

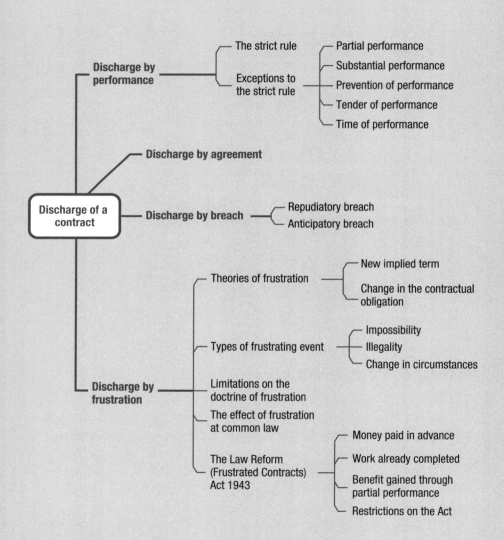

◼ Introduction

A contract is said to be discharged when it comes to an end.

A contract normally comes to an end when the obligations arising under it are performed. However, under certain circumstances, a contract may be discharged before performance is complete. This chapter will consider discharge by *performance* as well as by *agreement,* where the parties to the contract may end it before it is completed, *breach,* where there is a failure to perform contractual obligations, and *frustration,* where an intervening event prevents performance of the contract.

ASSESSMENT ADVICE

Issues covered in this chapter could arise as an essay question or form part of a problem question.

Essay questions

Although any of the topics in this chapter could be assessed, essay questions on frustration are particularly popular with examiners, so make sure that you revise this topic in depth. Be sure that you can outline the elements of the doctrine and make reference to relevant case law to support your explanation. In particular, you should be able to address the issue of whether it is acceptable that an otherwise binding contractual obligation can be avoided simply because unexpected events have made the contract less desirable.

Problem questions

Problem questions often combine issues raised by the discharge of a contract in conjunction with other topics. Look out for facts that trigger a discussion of these topics – for example, has work been left partially complete (performance), has only part of an order of goods been delivered (performance), how has the innocent party responded to a failure to complete performance (breach) and have any unexpected events occurred that have rendered performance of the contract more difficult than expected (frustration)?

◼ Sample question

Could you answer this question? Below is a typical essay question that could arise on this topic. Guidelines on answering the question are included at the end of the chapter, while a sample problem question and guidance on tackling it can be found on the companion website.

ESSAY QUESTION

'The object of the doctrine (of frustration) was to give effect to the demands of justice, to achieve a just and reasonable result, to do what is reasonable and fair, as an expedient to escape from injustice where such would result from enforcement of a contract in its literal terms after a significant change in circumstances . . .'

Bingham LJ in *J. Lauritzen AS* v *Wijsmuller BV (The Super Servant Two)* [1990] 1 Lloyd's Rep 1

Critically analyse this statement.

Discharge by performance

Strictly speaking, a contract is not discharged until all the obligations arising under it have been performed precisely and exactly.

The strict rule

Although this rule seems to make perfect common sense, it originated in relation to 'entire' contracts that require complete performance of all obligations and can give rise to harsh consequences:

KEY CASE

Cutter v *Powell* (1795) 6 Term Rep 320

Concerning: discharge by performance

Facts

A seaman agreed to serve on a ship. His wages were to be paid at the end of the voyage. He died mid-voyage. His widow attempted to claim his wages.

Legal principle

His widow was not able to recover any of his wages because he had not completed performance of his contractual obligation. (This situation is now provided for by the Merchant Shipping Act 1970.)

This principle has also led to harshness in contracts for the sale of goods:

KEY CASE

***Re Moore & Co's and Landauer & Co's Arbitration* [1921] 2 KB 519**

Concerning: discharge by performance

Facts

The defendants agreed to buy 3,000 tins of canned fruit from the claimants, packed in cases of 30 tins. Part of the consignment was in fact packed in cases of 24 tins. The defendants refused to pay.

Legal principle

The court held that the defendants were entitled to reject the entire consignment as it was not precisely that which was agreed.

This harshness has also now been mitigated by statute, in relation to non-consumer contracts for the sale of goods, by the following two provisions inserted into the Sale of Goods Act 1979 by the Sale and Supply of Goods Act 1994:

KEY STATUTE

Sale of Goods Act 1979, section 15A

Where in the case of a contract of sale –

(a) the buyer would . . . have the right to reject goods by reason of a breach on the part of the seller of a term implied by section 13, 14 or 15 above, but

(b) the breach is so slight that it would be unreasonable for him to reject them,

then, if the buyer does not deal as consumer, the breach is not to be treated as a breach of condition but may be treated as a breach of warranty.

KEY STATUTE

Sale of Goods Act 1979, section 30(2A)

A buyer who does not deal as consumer may not –

(a) where the seller delivers a quantity of goods less than he contracted to sell, reject the goods . . . , or ▶

(b) where the seller delivers a quantity of goods larger than he contracted to sell, reject the whole . . . ,

if the shortfall or, as the case may be, excess is so slight that it would be unreasonable for him to do so.

Given the potential for the strict application of the rule to create seemingly unfair results, the courts have developed exceptions to the rule.

Exceptions to the strict rule

Exceptions to the strict rule exist in relation to contracts which impose **severable obligations**.

KEY DEFINITION: Severable obligations

A contract imposes severable obligations if payment under it is due from time to time as performance of a specified part of the contract is rendered.

> G.H. Treitel, *The Law of Contract* (Sweet & Maxwell, London, 2003) 784

Whether or not a contract is severable is a question of interpretation for the court to decide. However, work and materials contracts are usually considered severable.

Partial performance

If a contract is severable, then, provided that the whole contract is not breached, payment can be expected for part performance.

KEY CASE

Roberts v *Havelock* **(1832) 3 B & Ad 404**

Concerning: discharge by performance; severable obligations

Facts

A shipwright agreed to repair a ship. The contract did not expressly state when payment was to be made. Before completing the repairs, he requested payment for the work completed to date. The defendants refused to pay.

> **Legal principle**
>
> Since the contract did not require the claimant to complete all the work before payment was made, the court held that the shipwright was not therefore bound to complete the repairs before claiming some payment.

Equally, partial performance may be accepted (*Christy* v *Row* (1808) 1 Taunt 300). Where partial performance is accepted (and the defendant has free choice whether or not to accept partial performance), then payment is enforceable in respect of the partial performance.

KEY CASE

> *Sumpter* v *Hedges* **[1898] 1 QB 673**
>
> *Concerning: discharge by performance; partial performance*
>
> **Facts**
>
> The claimant agreed to build a house and stables on the defendant's land. He completed around two-thirds of the work and then abandoned the contract. The defendant completed the buildings and refused to pay the claimant for the work done.
>
> **Legal principle**
>
> The claim failed. The claimant could not recover for the work done since the defendant had no option but to accept the partially completed building.

Substantial performance

Where performance is 'substantial', the contract may be enforced, although damages may be payable in respect of the incomplete performance. In other words, the amount payable corresponds to the price of the contract minus the cost of the incomplete component:

KEY CASE

> *H. Dakin & Co Ltd* v *Lee* **[1916] 1 KB 566**
>
> *Concerning: discharge by performance; substantial performance*
>
> **Facts**
>
> The claimants agreed to carry out repairs to the defendant's house. The work was completed but for three minor defects which could be fixed at a small cost. The defendant refused to pay. ▶

Legal principle

The court upheld the claim since the obligations under the contract had been substantially completed, subject to a deduction of the cost of fixing the outstanding defects.

However, this does give rise to the question of what exactly constitutes 'substantial' performance of contractual obligations. This is a question of fact in each case:

KEY CASE

Bolton v *Mahadeva* [1972] 2 All ER 1322

Concerning: discharge by performance; substantial performance

Facts

The claimant contracted to install a hot water and central heating system in the defendant's home for £560. There were numerous defects: fumes affected the air in the living room, the house was on average 10 per cent less warm than it should have been, and the deficiency in heat varied from room to room. Overall, it would cost £175 to rectify the deficiencies. At first instance, the judge held that the claimant was entitled to the agreed price of £560, but that £175 should be set off against the contract price because of the deficiencies. The defendant appealed.

Legal principle

The Court of Appeal held that there had *not* been substantial performance and therefore the claimant was not entitled to recover anything.

✎ EXAM TIP

When dealing with a problem question, look at the facts and ascertain what was required for complete performance of the contract. This can be used as a benchmark against which to measure what the defendant has actually done; you can then ask, 'How far short of the contractual obligation did the defendant fall?' This will enable you to determine whether there has been substantial performance.

Prevention of performance

Where a party is wrongly prevented from performing its contractual obligations by the other party then the strict rule does not apply. The claimant can either claim damages for **breach of contract** or on a **quantum meruit** basis for the work done (*Planché* v *Colburn* (1831) 8 Bing 14).

Tender of performance

If a party is unable to complete its contractual obligations without the co-operation of the other party, then it may make a 'tender of performance' which can be accepted or rejected by the other party. If a tender of performance is rejected, then the party who has tried to complete their contractual obligations will be discharged from further liability.

> **KEY CASE**
>
> ***Startup* v *MacDonald* (1843) 6 Man & C 593**
>
> *Concerning: discharge by performance; tender of performance*
>
> **Facts**
>
> The parties contracted for the sale of 10 tons of linseed oil to be delivered 'within the last 14 days of March'. The claimant delivered the oil at 8.30 p.m. on 31 March and the defendant refused to accept delivery. The defendant subsequently refused to pay.
>
> **Legal principle**
>
> The claim was successful. The court held that the tender of performance was equivalent to performance and the claimant was entitled to damages for non-acceptance. (Note that now section 29(5) of the Sale of Goods Act 1979 provides that a tender of goods must be made at a 'reasonable' hour – what is reasonable is a question of fact.)

Time of performance

Where a contract fixes a date for performance, it will still only be possible for the contract to be repudiated for breach of the time clause where 'time is of the essence'. This will occur where:

- the contract expressly provides that time is of the essence;
- time being of the essence can be inferred from the nature of the subject matter and the circumstances of the contract (e.g. a contract for the sale of perishable fresh fruit);
- time becomes of the essence: this happens where one party fails to perform in a timely manner and the injured party gives notice that performance must take place within a reasonable time.

If time is of the essence, any delay will amount to repudiation: in *Union Eagle Ltd* v *Golden Achievement Ltd* [1997] AC 514 the Privy Council considered that even a 10-minute delay would suffice.

■ Discharge by agreement

Just as a contract can be made by agreement, so it may also be discharged by agreement. However, in general, consideration is required to enforce the agreement to discharge or vary the contract. In some cases, certain formalities will also be required.

📖 **REVISION NOTE**

You may wish to review your understanding of consideration at this stage. See Chapter 2.

Where consideration is wholly executory (exchanged promises to perform some act in the future) then there is no problem. The parties' exchanged promises to release one another from the contract will be good consideration.

Where consideration is executed (either in part or wholly) then:

- a deed is required to effect a valid release of the other party; or
- the other party must provide 'accord and satisfaction' (that is, new consideration).

Alternatively, one party could give a voluntary (that is, without consideration) *waiver* to the other not to insist on the precise performance stipulated in the contract. A waiver can be given without formality.

■ Discharge by breach

KEY DEFINITION: Breach of contract

A breach of contract is committed when a party without lawful excuse fails or refuses to perform what is due from them under the contract, or performs defectively or incapacitates themselves from performing.

G.H. Treitel, *The Law of Contract* (Sweet & Maxwell, London, 2003) 832

📖 **REVISION NOTE**

It would be useful at this stage to consolidate your revision of the consequences of the breach of conditions, warranties and innominate terms. See Chapter 4.

Repudiatory breach

Repudiatory breaches are serious breaches that entitle the innocent party to consider themselves as being discharged from his obligations under the contract. This is in addition to the standard remedy of damages. In respect of a repudiatory breach, the innocent party may:

■ accept the breach as repudiation of the contract; or

■ affirm the breach (and continue with the contract).

If the breach is treated as repudiatory, this must be communicated to the party in breach of contract (*Vitol SA* v *Norelf Ltd* [1996] 3 All ER 193).

Anticipatory breach

Anticipatory breaches occur before performance is due. In essence, an anticipatory breach is where one party makes the other aware of their intention not to perform their contractual obligations. This may be:

■ explicitly (*Hochester* v *De La Tour* (1853) 2 E & B 678); or

■ implied by conduct (*Frost* v *Knight* (1872) LR 7 Exch 111).

The innocent party may either accept the repudiation and sue immediately, or wait for the contractual date of performance and sue for breach (if it occurs) in the usual way.

▉ Discharge by frustration

> **KEY DEFINITION: Doctrine of frustration**
>
> Under the doctrine of frustration a contract may be discharged if, after its formation, events occur making its performance impossible or illegal and in certain analogous situations.
>
> G.H. Treitel, *The Law of Contract* (Sweet & Maxwell, London, 2003) 866

Historically, contractual obligations were absolute:

> **KEY CASE**
>
> *Paradine* v *Jane* (1647) Aleyn 26
>
> *Concerning: frustration; absolute obligations*   ▶

Facts

Jane owed rent under a lease to Paradine. Jane contended that he had been forced off the land for three years during the term of the lease by an invading army and that he should not therefore be liable to pay rent.

Legal principle

The court held that there was still a contractual duty to pay rent. This was not discharged by the intervening event of the invasion. The court's view was that liability for intervening events should be covered by express provision for them in the contract.

The courts developed the **doctrine of frustration** in order to be fairer to parties whose failure to perform was beyond their control. If a contract is frustrated then it ends at the moment that the intervening event prevented performance.

Theories of frustration

There are two main theories behind the doctrine of frustration:

- that there is a new term implied into the contract; or
- that the obligation under the contract has changed.

New implied term

This was considered in *Taylor* v *Caldwell* (1863) 32 LJ QB 164 in which Blackburn J stated:

In contracts which depend on the continued existence of a given person or thing, a condition is implied that the impossibility of performance arising from the perishing of the person or thing shall excuse the performance . . . That excuse is by law implied, because from the nature of the contract it is apparent that the parties contracted on the basis of the continued existence of the particular person or chattel.

Change in the contractual obligation

The implied term theory was criticised for its artificiality. The theory that is now generally preferred is that propounded in *Davis Contractors Ltd* v *Fareham UDC* [1958] AC 696. Here Lord Radcliffe set out the test for frustration as follows:

. . . there must be a change in the significance of the obligation that the thing undertaken would, if performed, be a different thing than that contracted for.

> **✎ EXAM TIP**
>
> An understanding of the theory behind a legal principle can make a valuable contribution to essays on a particular topic so it is worth taking time to ensure that you have grasped these different theoretical perspectives on frustration. Remember, though, that such a discussion is appropriate only in an essay and has no place in a problem answer.

Types of frustrating event

There are three main classes of situation in which a contract might become frustrated:

- impossibility
- illegality
- change in circumstances.

Impossibility

There are a number of events that can lead to a situation in which it is impossible to perform a contract:

Event	Case
The subject matter of the contract is destroyed	*Taylor* v *Caldwell* (1863) 32 LJ QB 164
The subject matter of the contract becomes unavailable	*Jackson* v *Union Marine Insurance Co Ltd* (1874) LR 10 CP 125
A person required for the performance of the contract becomes unavailable through illness	*Robinson* v *Davidson* (1871) LR 6 Ex 269
A person required for the performance of the contract becomes unavailable for other good reason	*Morgan* v *Manser* [1948] 1 KB 184
There is an unavoidable excessive delay	*Pioneer Shipping Ltd* v *BTP Tioxide Ltd (The Nema)* [1981] 2 All ER 1030

Illegality

A contract may also become frustrated if there is a change in the law that makes the contract illegal to perform in the way that was anticipated in the contract. The courts do not expect parties to be contractually bound to do something illegal. The main cases here arose in wartime when laws are subject to change (such as the requisitioning of goods) to meet unusual circumstances: *Denny, Mott & Dickson Ltd* v *James B. Fraser & Co Ltd* [1944] 1 All ER 678 concerned the commercial sale of timber that was needed for the war effort; *Shipton Anderson & Co* v *Harrison Bros & Co* [1915] 3 KB 676 concerned the requisitioning of grain.

Change in circumstances

Contracts may also be frustrated where there is an event that destroys the central purpose of the contract such that all its commercial purpose is destroyed.

KEY CASE

Krell v *Henry* [1903] 2 KB 740

Concerning: frustration; frustration of purpose

Facts

Henry hired a room from Krell for two days in order to view the coronation procession of Edward VII, but the contract itself made no reference to that intended use. The King's illness caused a postponement of the procession. The defendant refused to pay for the room.

Legal principle

The court held that the contract was frustrated. Henry was excused from paying the rent for the room. The holding of the procession on the dates planned was regarded as the foundation of the contract.

For the contract to be frustrated in this way, all commercial purpose must have been destroyed. If there is some purpose to be found in the contract then it will continue. An example of this can be found in another case which came about from Edward VII's postponed coronation:

KEY CASE

Herne Bay Steamboat Co v *Hutton* [1903] 2 KB 683

Concerning: frustration; frustration of purpose

Facts

The defendant hired a boat to sail around the Solent to see the new King's inspection of the fleet that was gathered in port and to see the fleet itself, which was seldom gathered in one place. The inspection was postponed.

Legal principle

The court held that the contract was not frustrated. Although one purpose (seeing the King's inspection of the fleet) had been destroyed, the defendant was still able to use the boat and see the fleet. The court considered that there was still some commercial value in the contract.

This also applies to leases (*National Carriers Ltd* v *Panalpina (Northern) Ltd* [1981] AC 675) where the purpose of the lease as foreseen by both parties has become impossible and there is therefore no purpose left in the lease.

Limitations on the doctrine of frustration

Although the courts developed the doctrine of frustration to mitigate the harshness from the strict common law position in *Paradine* v *Jane,* it might still lead to unfair results. The courts have therefore identified certain situations in which the doctrine of frustration does *not* apply:

Situation	Case
The frustration is self-induced	*J. Lauritzen AS* v *Wijsmuller BV (The Super Servant Two)* [1990] 1 Lloyd's Rep 1
The contract has merely become more difficult to perform or less beneficial to one of the parties	*Davis Contractors Ltd* v *Fareham UDC* [1958] AC 696
The frustrating event was in the contemplation of the parties at the time that the contract was formed (or the parties should have contemplated that it might occur)	*Amalgamated Investment & Property Co Ltd* v *John Walker & Sons Ltd* [1977] 1 WLR 164
There were provisions in the contract for the frustrating event which covered the extent of the loss or damage caused	*Fibrosa Spolka Akcyjna* v *Fairbairn Lawson Combe Barbour Ltd* [1943] AC 32
The contract expressly provides that performance should occur under any circumstances	*Paradine* v *Jane* (1647) Aleyn 26

The effect of frustration at common law

At common law, the contract ends at the actual point at which it is frustrated – that is, from the frustrating event. Therefore the parties are released from any contractual obligations from that point forward. However, they are still bound by any obligations that arose before the contract was frustrated (see Figure 8.1).

Figure 8.1

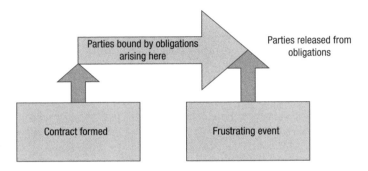

However, this can lead to unfairness. The outcome of frustration of a contract would depend entirely on the point in the contract at which frustration took place. This can be illustrated by yet another case arising from the delayed coronation of Edward VII:

KEY CASE

Chandler v *Webster* [1904] 1 KB 493

Concerning: frustration; strict common law rule

Facts

As in *Krell* v *Henry*, the claimant rented a hotel room from the defendant to watch the coronation of King Edward VII. He paid a deposit and agreed to pay the balance on the day. After the cancellation of the coronation, the claimant argued that the contract was frustrated, and claimed the return of his deposit.

Legal principle

As in *Krell* v *Henry*, the court held that the contract was frustrated. However, the crucial difference here is that the room was paid for in advance (*before* the frustrating event), whereas in *Krell* v *Henry* it was to be paid on the day of the coronation procession. The court therefore would not allow the claimant to recover the money already paid.

The House of Lords modified this position in an attempt to mitigate the harshness of the strict common law rule:

KEY CASE

Fibrosa Spolka Akcyjna v *Fairbairn Lawson Combe Barbour Ltd* **[1943] AC 32**

Concerning: frustration; modified common law rule

Facts

A contract for manufacture and delivery of machinery to a Polish company was frustrated by the invasion of Poland, which precipitated the Second World War. The Polish company had made a contractual advance payment of £1,000.

Legal principle

The House of Lords held that a party *could* recover payments made prior to a frustrating event, provided that there was a total failure of consideration. *Per* Lord Macmillan:

> Owing to circumstances arising out of present hostilities the contract has become impossible of fulfilment according to its terms. Neither party is to blame. In return for their money the plaintiffs [now claimants] have received nothing whatever from the defendants by way of fulfilment of any part of the contract. It is thus a typical case of a total failure of consideration. The money paid must be repaid.

This is an improvement over the position from *Chandler* v *Webster*. However, it is still not ideal – for instance, in *Fibrosa* the manufacturer received no payment for any work that it had done in advance of the contract. As a result, Parliament, following *Fibrosa,* intervened with statute in the form of the Law Reform (Frustrated Contracts) Act 1943.

The Law Reform (Frustrated Contracts) Act 1943

The Act deals with three areas:

■ recovery of money paid in advance;
■ recovery of work already completed;
■ recovery for a benefit gained through partial performance.

Money paid in advance

This provision confirms the *Fibrosa* principle that money already paid is recoverable and that money due under the contract ceases to be payable (as in *Taylor* v *Caldwell*).

KEY STATUTE

Law Reform (Frustrated Contracts) Act 1943, section 1(2)

All sums paid or payable to any party in pursuance of the contract before the time when the parties were so discharged (in this Act referred to as 'the time of discharge') shall, in the case of sums so paid, be recoverable from him as money received by him for the use of the party by whom the sums were paid, and, in the case of sums so payable, cease to be so payable:

Provided that, if the party to whom the sums were so paid or payable incurred expenses before the time of discharge in, or for the purpose of, the performance of the contract, the court may, if it considers it just to do so having regard to all the circumstances of the case, allow him to retain or, as the case may be, recover the whole or any part of the sums so paid or payable, not being an amount in excess of the expenses so incurred.

Work already completed

Under section 1(2) the court also has discretion to reward a party who has already carried out work under or in preparation for the contract. However, this is discretionary and therefore does not automatically guarantee that all actual expenses will be recoverable (*Gamerco SA v ICM/Fair Warning Agency* [1995] 1 WLR 1226).

Benefit gained through partial performance

Section 1(3) of the Act considers recovery for partial performance:

KEY STATUTE

Law Reform (Frustrated Contracts) Act 1943, section 1(3)

Where any party to the contract has, by reason of anything done by any other party thereto in, or for the purpose of, the performance of the contract, obtained a valuable benefit (other than a payment of money to which the last foregoing subsection applies) before the time of discharge, there shall be recoverable from him by the said other party such sum (if any), not exceeding the value of the said benefit to the party obtaining it, as the court considers just, having regard to all the circumstances of the case and, in particular, –

(a) the amount of any expenses incurred before the time of discharge by the benefited party in, or for the purpose of, the performance of the contract, including any sums paid or payable by him to any other party in pursuance of the contract and retained or recoverable by that party under the last foregoing subsection, and

(b) the effect, in relation to the said benefit, of the circumstances giving rise to the frustration of the contract.

Therefore, the court must first consider whether a valuable benefit has been conferred. Having established this, the court must consider a just sum to award in all the circumstances. In essence, this discretion exists to prevent unjust enrichment of one of the parties (*BP Exploration Co (Libya) Ltd* v *Hunt (No. 2)* [1979] 1 WLR 783).

Restrictions on the Act

The Act specifically excludes certain circumstances:

Circumstance	Section
The contract is severable and one part has been completely performed. The court treats the severable part as though it were separate	2(4)
Carriage of goods by sea (except time charter-parties)	2(5)(a)
Contracts of insurance	2(5)(b)
Perishing of goods under section 7 of the Sale of Goods Act 1979	2(5)(c)

■ Putting it all together

Answer guidelines

See the sample question at the start of the chapter.

Approaching the question

This is an essay question focusing on frustration of contract that is based upon a quotation from one of the leading cases. The quotation addresses the objective of the doctrine of frustration which is to achieve fairness and to avoid the injustice that would arise from strict enforcement of a contract following some unforeseen event that was not the fault of the parties.

Important points to include

- The quotation suggests that the predominant concern of the doctrine of frustration is to achieve a fair result, so it would be useful to start your essay by explaining how the law was unfair in the first place. The most effective way of explaining the

▶

harshness that results from the imposition of an absolute obligation would be to do so by reference to *Paradine* v *Jane*.

- You should explain that there are three main ways in which a contract may become frustrated: impossibility, illegality and change of circumstances. Deal with each of these in turn and support your answer with examples from case law.

- It would be important to point out that the doctrine may still lead to unfair results and to show how the courts have developed exceptions in which they have held that the doctrine does not apply.

- Discuss how the operation of frustration at common law could lead to harsh results such as the parties being bound by obligations prior to the frustration (*Chandler* v *Webster*) and explain how this led to the modification in *Fibrosa* and ultimately the enactment of the Law Reform (Frustrated Contracts) Act 1943.

- Remember that you should draw the strands of your argument together into a cohesive and coherent conclusion that addresses the quotation directly and provides a focused answer to the question. On balance, in light of the points you have discussed, does the law meet its objective of achieving fairness and avoiding harsh results?

 Make your answer stand out

- Make sure that your essay has a strong focus. This means that it should not just be about frustration but that it should make points that address the issues about frustration (fairness and the avoidance of injustice) raised by the question. For example, when providing examples of each of the situations in which a contract may be frustrated, use examples from case law and then link these to the question by explaining how the outcome of the case would be unfair without the doctrine of frustration. This slant will strengthen your focus and create a far more effective answer to the question.

- Do not neglect the provisions of the Law Reform (Frustrated Contracts) Act 1943. These are often overlooked by students who either fail to mention the statutory position at all or dismiss it in a sentence without explaining how it relates to the common law. Avoid this common problem by outlining the provisions of the Act and its restrictions. Consider whether the limitations established by statute mean that there are still situations in which the outcome of frustration may lead to unfairness.

READ TO IMPRESS

Brodie, D. (2006) Performance issues and frustration of contract. *Employment Law Bulletin,* 71: 4.

Reynolds, F. (1981) Discharge of contract by breach. *Law Quarterly Review,* 97: 541.

Trakman, L. (1983) Frustrated contracts and legal fictions. *Modern Law Review,* 47: 39.

Treitel, G. (2004) *Frustration and Force Majeure,* 2nd revd edn. London: Sweet & Maxwell.

www.pearsoned.co.uk/lawexpress

Go online to access more revision support including quizzes to test your knowledge, sample questions with answer guidelines, podcasts you can download, and more!

Remedies

■ Topic map

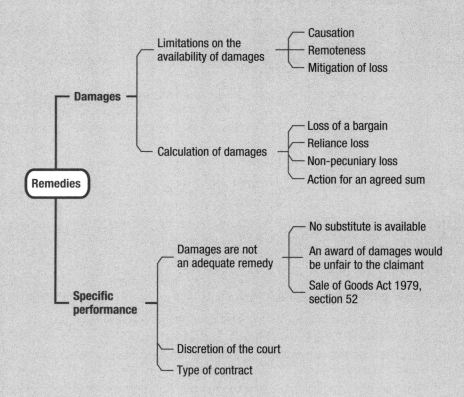

- **Remedies**
  - **Damages**
    - Limitations on the availability of damages
      - Causation
      - Remoteness
      - Mitigation of loss
    - Calculation of damages
      - Loss of a bargain
      - Reliance loss
      - Non-pecuniary loss
      - Action for an agreed sum
  - **Specific performance**
    - Damages are not an adequate remedy
      - No substitute is available
      - An award of damages would be unfair to the claimant
      - Sale of Goods Act 1979, section 52
    - Discretion of the court
    - Type of contract

A printable version of this topic map is available from **www.pearsoned.co.uk/lawexpress**

■ Introduction

Although you will often be asked whether a party can 'enforce the contract', the most usual remedy is not specific performance, which would compel the party in breach to fulfil their contractual obligations, but damages.

Damages are a common law remedy and are available as of right if there has been a breach of contract. This chapter will explore the limitations on the availability of damages – issues of causation and remoteness and the duty to mitigate loss – as well as looking at methods for calculating damages. It will also consider the tricky issue of damages that cover non-pecuniary loss. These issues are important as you need to be able to assess not only whether there is a claim for breach of contract but also what the innocent party is likely to receive as a result of that breach. The chapter will move on to consider specific performance. As this is an equitable remedy, it is available at the discretion of the court, so it is important that you are able to identify the circumstances in which the courts will compel the party in breach to continue with the performance of the contract.

ASSESSMENT ADVICE

Issues covered in this chapter could arise as an essay question or form part of a problem question.

Essay questions

Essay questions focusing on remedies are not popular with students although they do appear on exam papers quite frequently. Such questions may specify that they are looking for a discussion of damages, e.g. 'Discuss the extent to which an award of damages is an adequate remedy for breach of contract' or may be phrased more generally: 'Assess what remedies are available following a breach of contract'. Make sure you know enough about the topic to do what the question requires. For example, it would be a mistake to attempt a question that asks whether damages are an adequate remedy if you could describe the different methods of calculating damages but were not able to identify situations in which they are not an adequate remedy.

Problem questions

Problem questions on damages often combine with some other topic so that the first part of the question requires that you establish that the contract has been breached and the second requires you to assess the extent of the claimant's damages. Alternatively, a question might state that breach is established and therefore leave only issues of the availability of remedies to be explored. Make sure that you read the question carefully and follow the instructions so that you do only what is required.

■ Sample question

Could you answer this question? Below is a typical problem question that could arise on this topic. Guidelines on answering the question are included at the end of the chapter, while a sample essay question and guidance on tackling it can be found on the companion website.

PROBLEM QUESTION

Sally has been made redundant from her job as a university lecturer. She enjoys cooking so decides to use her redundancy payment to start her own catering business. She enters into a contract with Alan, which stipulates that he will convert her garage into a large kitchen and install commercial catering equipment. The contract specifies that the work must be completed within four weeks.

Alan commences work and Sally sets about generating interest in her new business. She spends £5,000 on promotional literature and advertising and she is pleased to receive a booking to cater for a silver wedding anniversary in five weeks' time. Sally tells Alan about the booking and checks to ensure that the work will be finished in time and Alan assures her that he is ahead of schedule. Sally receives an enquiry from a local business about the provision of executive lunches for 12 people every weekday and enters into negotiations to secure this contract.

Three days prior to the date agreed for completion of the kitchen, Alan admits to Sally that the work is hopelessly behind schedule and that it is likely to take him another four weeks to complete the kitchen. Sally has to cancel the anniversary booking. News of this reaches the local business and they contact Sally to tell her that they have no interest in engaging her services because she is unreliable. Sally has a breakdown due to the stress caused by the failure of her business.

Advise Sally as to the extent of her claim in damages against Alan.

■ Damages

KEY DEFINITION: Damages

Damages are a financial remedy that aims to compensate the injured party for the consequences of the breach of contract. In general, the principle that guides the award of damages is that the injured party should be put into the position, as far as is possible, that they would have been in if the contract had been carried out.

The aim of an award of **damages** is to ensure that the innocent party does not suffer as a result of the other party's breach of contract but is put in the same position that they would have been in had the other party honoured their contractual obligations. It is important to remember that contractual damages are restorative not punitive, *per* Lord Atkinson in *Addis* v *Gramophone Co Ltd* [1909] AC 488:

> I have always understood that damages for breach of contract were in the nature of compensation, not punishment.

Limitations on the availability of damages

It might seem logical to expect that an innocent party that can establish that the other contracting party has breached the contract would be able to claim damages but there are three factors to take into account that may limit the availability of damages:

- causation
- remoteness
- mitigation of loss.

Causation

A claimant can recover damages only if the breach of contract caused his loss. It is not enough that there is breach of contract and loss: the loss must be a consequence of the breach. As such, an intervening act that occurs between the breach of contract and the loss may breach the chain of causation (see Figure 9.1).

Figure 9.1

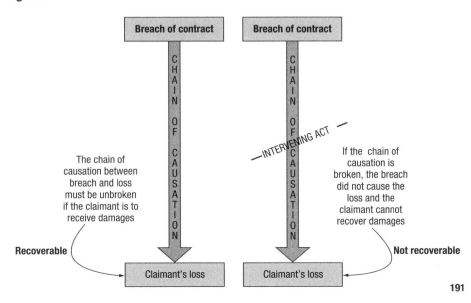

KEY CASE

County Ltd v *Girozentrale Securities* [1996] 3 All ER 834

Concerning: chain of causation, intervening acts

Facts

The claimant bank underwrote the issue of 26 million shares in an oil exploration company. The defendant was a firm of stockbrokers engaged by the claimant to find investors interested in the shares. The defendant set about finding investors but acted outside the terms of their agreement with the claimant and, as a result of this and other factors, many of the shares were unsold. The claimant brought an action to recover the loss, which was in the region of £7 million.

Legal principle

The Court of Appeal upheld the claimant's appeal on the basis that the defendant had acted outside their instructions and that this breach of contract was an effective cause of the claimant's loss. It was immaterial that other factors, including the claimant's own conduct, contributed to the loss.

As such, it is clear that the breach of conduct may be a cause of the loss, i.e. one of several causes, rather than *the* cause, i.e. the sole cause of loss.

✎ EXAM TIP

It is important that you remember to mention causation in your answer to a problem question on this topic. Even though the issue of causation is not usually complicated when it arises in a problem question, many students omit to mention it at all. It is important to cover causation so that your answer is complete and so that you can attract marks for dealing with this often forgotten issue.

Remoteness

Causation is the first hurdle that must be cleared in order for the injured party to recover damages from the party in breach but, having done this, it is then necessary to establish that the loss, even though caused by the breach, was not too remote from it. In other words, not all loss that is caused by breach of contract is recoverable.

KEY CASE

Hadley v *Baxendale* (1854) 9 Ex 341

Concerning: damages and remoteness

Facts

The claimants owned a mill. A crankshaft, which was essential for the operation of the mill, broke and needed to be replaced using the original as a template. The claimants engaged the defendants, a firm of carriers, to transport the broken part to engineers in Greenwich where a replacement would be made but the defendants failed to do this within the time frame specified thus delaying the arrival of the new part and causing the mill to stand inoperative. The claimants sought damages to compensate for the losses sustained while the mill was idle.

Legal principle

The Court of Exchequer accepted the defendant's submission that the loss was too remote and should not be recoverable. It would have been an entirely different position if the defendants had been made aware that the mill would be inoperable without the part but they were not aware that this was the only crankshaft that the claimant possessed.

This judgment gave rise to the foreseeability test (*per* Alderson B):

Where two parties have made a contract which one of them has broken, the damages which the other party ought to receive in respect of such breach of contract should be such as may fairly and reasonably be considered either arising naturally, i.e., according to the usual course of things, from such breach of contract itself, or such as may reasonably be supposed to have been in the contemplation of both parties at the time they made the contract as the probable result of the breach of it.

This creates two situations in which the requirements of remoteness will be satisfied that are referred to as the two limbs of the *Hadley* v *Baxendale* test of foreseeability (see Figure 9.2).

Figure 9.2

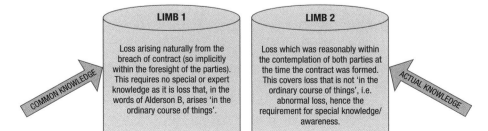

LIMB 1

Loss arising naturally from the breach of contract (so implicitly within the foresight of the parties). This requires no special or expert knowledge as it is loss that, in the words of Alderson B, arises 'in the ordinary course of things'.

COMMON KNOWLEDGE

LIMB 2

Loss which was reasonably within the contemplation of both parties at the time the contract was formed. This covers loss that is not 'in the ordinary course of things', i.e. abnormal loss, hence the requirement for special knowledge/ awareness.

ACTUAL KNOWLEDGE

9 REMEDIES

The *Hadley* v *Baxendale* principle was considered in two subsequent cases:

KEY CASE

Victoria Laundry Ltd v *Newman Industries* [1949] 2 KB 528

Concerning: remoteness, loss within the contemplation of the parties

Facts

The claimants ran a laundry business. They purchased a boiler from the defendants that was due for delivery in July. The boiler sustained some damage and had to be repaired which delayed delivery until November. The claimants had made the defendants aware that they needed the boiler to expand their business and that they wanted it for immediate use. They claimed damages to represent the loss of ordinary profits that would have been made from their additional business if the boiler had arrived as agreed and also for the loss of government contracts that they had intended to secure once the boiler arrived.

Legal principle

It was held that the claimants could recover damages for the loss of additional profit but not for the loss of revenue from the government contracts. This was because the defendants were aware that the claimants aimed to increase their business by acquiring another boiler, thus the loss of the additional income was a 'reasonably foreseeable' consequence of breach, whereas there was nothing to suggest that the defendants were aware of the claimants' plans concerning government contracts so this was not recoverable.

Victoria Laundry provides an example of the operation of the second limb and sets the standard of remoteness as 'reasonable foreseeability' but the House of Lords disagreed with this level of probability in *The Heron II*:

KEY CASE

The Heron II [1969] 1 AC 350

Concerning: remoteness, loss within the contemplation of the parties

Facts

The claimant chartered *The Heron II* to transport a cargo of sugar on a journey that should have taken 20 days but actually, due to a deviation from the route by the defendant,

---

took 29 days during which the price of sugar fell significantly. The late arrival put the defendant in breach of contract so the claimant sought damages to cover the difference in the price he received for the sugar and the higher price that he would have received had the boat arrived on time. The claimant had not told the defendant that he intended to sell the sugar at the destination but the defendant was aware that he was carrying sugar and that the destination was a popular trading place for sugar.

Legal principle

The House of Lords held that, although the claimant had not told the defendant that he intended to sell the sugar as soon as the boat arrived, the defendant's knowledge that he was carrying sugar and his awareness that the destination was a popular trading place for sugar was sufficient to make it so probable that it must have been within his contemplation at the time the contract was made. The House of Lords criticised the reference to 'reasonable foresight' in *Victoria Laundry,* as this is a term that is more appropriate in tort, with Lord Reid stating:

> The question for decision is whether a [claimant] can recover as damages for breach of contract a loss of the kind which the defendant, when he made the contract, ought to have realised was not unlikely to result from a breach of contract . . . I use the words 'not unlikely' as denoting a degree of probability considerably less than an even chance but nevertheless not very unusual and easily foreseeable.

EXAM TIP

Remember that if you are dealing with this issue in a problem question, you will need to state the legal principle established in *Hadley* v *Baxendale* and refer to examples of the rule in operation in cases such as *Victoria Laundry* or *The Heron II*. However, if you were revising this topic in preparation for an essay question, you would need a more detailed understanding of the judicial reasoning in each of these cases plus the ability to engage in critical comment on the way in which the law has developed. You might find it useful to read an article which discusses remoteness and its treatment in case law, such as Tettenborn's (2003) article, to give you some ideas for critical analysis in an essay.

Finally, provided that the type of loss caused by the breach is within the reasonable contemplation of the parties, the magnitude of that loss does not have to be (*H. Parsons (Livestock) Ltd* v *Uttley Ingham & Co Ltd* [1978] 1 QB 791; *Transfield Shipping Inc* v *Mercator Shipping Inc (The Achilleas)* [2008] UKHL 48).

Mitigation of loss

The third factor to take into account when considering the availability and quantification of damages is the **duty to mitigate**.

> **KEY DEFINITION: The duty to mitigate**
>
> The duty to mitigate refers to a principle of contract law whereby the innocent party who has suffered a breach of contract has a duty to take reasonable steps to minimise the extent of their loss arising from the breach.

The innocent victim of a breach of contract will be entitled to damages to cover losses caused by the breach that are not too remote provided he has not failed to take action that would have reduced the extent of his losses.

> **KEY CASE**
>
> ***Brace** v **Calder** [1895] 2 QB 253*
>
> *Concerning: duty to take reasonable steps to mitigate loss*
>
> **Facts**
>
> The claimant was offered employment for a period of two years. After five months, the company was dissolved due to the retirement of two of its owners which cut short the claimant's employment. However, two of the owners continued the business in their own right and offered the claimant employment which he refused.
>
> **Legal principle**
>
> His claim for damages to cover the loss of earnings for the remainder of the two-year period was refused on the basis that he had failed to take advantage of the opportunity to reduce his losses by accepting the offer of employment.

The key point to remember here is to think about what it was reasonable for the claimant to do in the circumstances to reduce the extent of his losses. This will depend on the factual circumstances involved in each situation. Note that it is only required that the claimant take reasonable steps to minimise his losses – the courts have held that a claimant should not be expected to take onerous measures to limit his loss.

KEY CASE

Pilkington v *Wood* [1953] 2 All ER 810

Concerning: duty to take reasonable steps to mitigate loss

Facts

The claimant bought a house but there was a defect in the title that meant that he was not able to take possession of the property for some time while the situation was rectified. The claimant's solicitor was in breach of contract for his failure to take appropriate steps to spot the defect in title; thus the claimant brought an action to recover damages relating to the costs of hotel bills and many other costs associated with the delay in the completion of the sale. The defendant solicitor argued that the claimant could have pursued the vendor of the property for these costs and that this would have been a reasonable measure to take to mitigate the losses arising from the solicitor's breach of contract.

Legal principle

The defendant's argument was rejected. A claim against the vendor would have required the claimant to pursue complicated litigation which may not have been successful whereas the breach of contract claim against the solicitor was straightforward. As such, it was not reasonable to expect the claimant to take the risk of pursuing the vendor so there was no duty to do so in order to mitigate the losses arising from the solicitor's breach of contract.

Calculation of damages

As damages are available as of right, the question is not whether the successful claimant will receive damages (they will be subject to issues of causation, remoteness and mitigation) but how the amount of damages payable is to be calculated. There are two methods of determining the extent of damages that will be awarded:

- Loss of a bargain: places the innocent party in the position they would have been in if the contract had been performed.

- Reliance loss: places the innocent party in the position they would have been in if the contract had never been made.

Each of these will be considered in more detail in the sections that follow.

Before doing so, it is important to note that, as the aim of damages is either to place the innocent party in the position they would have been in if the contract had been performed (loss of bargain) or if the contract had never been made (reliance loss), a defendant who has neither spent nor lost money cannot recover damages. For example, if Tom agrees to sell his car to Chris but Chris changes his mind and refuses to pay, he is in breach of contract.

If Tom is able to sell the car for the same or higher price to James, Tom has lost nothing as a result of Chris's breach so would receive only *nominal damages,* i.e. a small sum to acknowledge the breach of contract.

Loss of a bargain

This is the main category of damages awarded for breach of contract. It is sometimes known as 'expectation loss' as the innocent party has lost what he expected to receive from the contract. As such, this form of damages aims to put the innocent party in the position that they would have been in if the contract had been performed.

There are two possible situations:

1. There is no performance by one of the parties to the contract. This could mean that the party who was bound to supply goods or services failed to do so or it could mean that the party who was due to receive goods or services refused to accept them. In this case, damages will represent the cost to the innocent party of obtaining the goods or services that should have been supplied. This may be the actual value of the contract if a substitute can be found at that price, or the market value of the goods/services which may be higher than the price agreed in the contract.

Substitute at actual value: *Charter* v *Sullivan* [1957] 1 QB 117	Substitute at market value: *WL Thompson Ltd* v *Robinson Gunmakers Ltd* [1955] Ch 177
In both of these cases, the defendant had agreed to purchase a car but subsequently refused to complete the transaction, thus putting himself in breach of contract.	
The claimant accepted that there was a good market for the car, thus it would not be difficult to obtain the same price from another purchaser. As such, the claimant had suffered no loss, so only nominal damages were awarded.	Here, there was less demand for the car in question and it was likely that it would be sold for a lower price than that agreed with the defendant. As such, the claimant was entitled to damages to reflect the loss of profit.

2. There is performance in the sense that goods or services are provided but these are defective or of an inferior quality to that stipulated by the contract. Here, damages will either cover the cost of restoring the goods to the expected quality (cost of cure) or represent the gap in the price between the goods expected (good quality/undamaged) and those received (inferior quality/defective) (difference in value). This may also raise issues of whether it is the actual value or market value that is the appropriate basis for calculation of damages.

KEY CASE

Ruxley Electronics and Construction Ltd v Forsyth [1995] 3 WLR 118

Concerning: basis for calculating damages

Facts

The claimant engaged the services of the defendant to construct a swimming pool at a cost of £70,000. When it was completed, the depth of the pool was several inches less than had been stipulated in the contract. The cost of rectifying the defect by rebuilding the swimming pool would have been over £20,000 (cost of cure) which would have imposed an unacceptable hardship on the defendant, given that the pool was perfectly functional in every other respect. The difference in depth made no difference to the value of the pool so the claimant received only nominal damages (although an award of £2,500 was made for loss of amenity).

Legal principle

The House of Lords emphasised that the aim of damages was to put the innocent party in the position they would have been in if the contract had been performed but ruled that this did not necessarily mean that the innocent party would be entitled to the monetary equivalent of specific performance.

However, the House of Lords has held that, in certain circumstances, restitutionary damages can be awarded.

KEY CASE

Attorney General v Blake [2000] 1 AC 268

Concerning: damages, restitution; account of profits

Facts

Blake was a member of MI6. He had signed a declaration under the Official Secrets Act 1911 not to disclose information about his work which applied even after his employment had finished. For 10 years he acted as a Soviet agent. He was imprisoned, but escaped and fled to the Soviet Union via Berlin. He wrote a book which was published in 1989 and for which he had received £60,000 in publisher's payments in advance with a further £90,000 due. The Crown commenced an action with a view to ensuring that Blake should not receive the further £90,000.

Legal principle

The House of Lords held that Blake must account for the profits earned by the publication of the book on his activities in breach of his contract with the government whereby he had agreed not to disclose information gained as a result of his employment. As Lord Nicholls commented: ▶

Remedies are the law's response to a wrong (or, more precisely, to a cause of action). When, exceptionally, a just response to a breach of contract so requires, the court should be able to grant the discretionary remedy of requiring a defendant to account to the [claimant] for the benefits he has received from his breach of contract. In the same way as a plaintiff's interest in performance of a contract may render it just and equitable for the court to make an order for specific performance [see the next section of this chapter] or grant an injunction, so the [claimant's] interest in performance may make it just and equitable that the defendant should retain no benefit from his breach of contract.

In *AB* v *CD* [2014] EWCA Civ 229 the Court of Appeal held that the existence of a limitation clause (as to the availability of damages on termination) cannot fetter a court's determination of whether damages will be adequate if a breach occurs.

Reliance loss

There are situations in which it is difficult or impossible to calculate damages on the basis of the position that the defendant would have been in if the contract had been performed so a different basis for calculation is used that focuses on loss caused by reliance on the contract. Here, the aim is to place the innocent party in the position that they would have been in if the contract had never been made.

KEY CASE

Anglia Television Ltd v *Reed* [1972] 1 QB 60

Concerning: calculation of reliance loss

Facts

The claimant television company entered into a contract with the actor, Robert Reed, to star in a film. Reed subsequently decided to take part in an American film and, as the filming would have clashed with the claimant's film, refused to go ahead, thus breaching his contract. As a result, the film was abandoned. The claimant sought to recover expenditure both before and after the contract was signed on the basis that this money was spent in reliance on the contract with the defendant.

Legal principle

It was uncomplicated to find that expenditure after the contract was formed was recoverable as it was reasonable to expect that the film company would spend money preparing for filming. It was less clear that damages were recoverable for expenditure incurred prior to the formation of the contract as it seemed less clear that these arose due to reliance on the contract as the contract did not exist at the time. However, it was held that there was no reason why costs incurred prior to the contract could not be recoverable provided that they were not too remote. As the defendant was aware that all costs associated with making the film would be wasted if the contract did not go ahead, the claimant was able to claim damages for money spent prior to the formation of the contract.

In *Anglia Television Ltd* v *Reed,* the Court of Appeal also stated that it was for the claimant to decide whether they wanted to claim for expectation loss or reliance loss.

Reliance loss provides a good basis for a claim of damages for claimants who cannot establish what, if anything, they have lost that falls within expectation loss. Here, for example, the film company did not seek damages for expectation loss based upon the profit that the film would have made as this would have been too difficult to predict.

However, claimants cannot claim for losses that would have occurred anyway if the contract had been properly performed. To allow this would be to put the claimant in a better position than he would have been in had the contract not been breached. Losses made as a result of a bad bargain would have happened regardless and come from the claimant agreeing the contract on unfavourable terms, not as a result of the defendant's breach (*C & P Haulage Co Ltd* v *Middleton* [1983] 1 WLR 1461; *Omak Maritime Ltd* v *Mamola Challenger Shipping Co (The Mamola Challenger)* [2010] EWHC 2026 (Comm)).

Non-pecuniary loss

Damages are an award of a sum of money that aims to put the innocent party in the position they would have been in if the contract had been performed (expectation loss) or not made (reliance loss) so it follows that the calculation of damages is most straightforward in relation to financial loss. For many years, damages were limited to pecuniary loss but it is now recognised that there are situations in which damages may be paid in relation to injury to feelings, mental distress and loss of amenity.

KEY CASE

Jarvis v *Swans Tours* **[1973] 1 All ER 71**

Concerning: damages for loss of enjoyment

Facts

The claimant booked a two-week holiday that specified certain features, such as a welcome party, afternoon tea and yodelling sessions. These features were either absent (the welcome party) or unsatisfactory (afternoon tea and yodelling). The holiday company was clearly in breach of contract for failing to provide these features but the issue ▶

was the extent to which the claimant could recover for their absence given that they amounted to loss of enjoyment rather than financial loss.

Legal principle

At first instance, the claimant recovered only a small sum to cover the cost of the features that he had not received, but on appeal his award was increased to reflect damages for the loss of enjoyment. The rationale for the decision was that the very purpose of a holiday is enjoyment; therefore, it followed that damages should be available if the level of enjoyment promised was not forthcoming.

This notion of identifying the very object or purpose of the contract and providing damages if that object is not provided also enables claimants to recover for the mental distress associated with the failure of the contract. This is applicable only to contracts where the essence of the contract is to provide pleasure: there can be no recovery for mental distress in purely commercial contracts.

Cases in which damages have been awarded for mental distress include:

- a sum awarded to represent the disappointment and anxiety caused by the non-appearance of a wedding photographer: *Diesen* v *Sampson* 1971 SLT 49;
- damages for mental distress arising from a solicitor's negligent failure to obtain an injunction to protect the claimant from molestation: *Heywood* v *Wellers* [1976] QB 446.

Damages may be awarded for loss of amenity as was the case in *Ruxley Electronics and Construction Ltd* v *Forsyth* (discussed above).

There are situations in which damages may be available in relation to the loss of chance caused by breach of contract:

- In *Blackpool and Fylde Aero Club* v *Blackpool Borough Council* [1990] 1 WLR 1195 damages were awarded to the claimant when Blackpool Borough Council failed to consider their application for a tender, as this had deprived them of the chance to win the contract, even though it was by no means certain that they would have done so.
- In *Chaplin* v *Hicks* [1911] 2 KB 786, the claimant received damages to represent the lost chance of success in a beauty contest even though her success was only a possibility, not a certainty.

Action for an agreed sum

If the price to be paid for performance of the contract is specified but payment is not forthcoming once performance has taken place, the innocent party may bring an action for an agreed sum. This is not the same as damages as the innocent party is seeking to enforce the contract by compelling the other party to pay rather than seeking compensation for loss suffered. The time at which payment is due will depend on the terms of the contract.

An action for an agreed sum is straightforward where a price is specified as there is no issue of remoteness and no need for quantification of damages. Difficulties arise if a price is not specified but there has been some performance of the contractual obligation. In such a situation, the price is calculated on a *quantum meruit* basis: that is, as much money as is deserved in relation to the work done. This is calculated on the basis of the market price for the work in question.

Specific performance

It is important to remember that damages are the main remedy for breach of contract. Damages are available as of right, i.e. once breach of contract is established, the injured party is entitled to an award of damages, whereas the availability of **specific performance** is limited on the basis of three considerations, each of which will be considered in turn:

- It is available only if damages are not an adequate remedy.
- As it is an equitable remedy, it is available at the discretion of the judge.
- It is available only for certain types of contract.

> **KEY DEFINITION: Specific performance**
>
> Specific performance is an equitable remedy that compels the party in breach to perform his part of the contract. It is generally positive in nature, i.e. it compels the party in breach to do something, as opposed to an injunction which is negative or prohibitory in nature, i.e. it compels a person to refrain from doing something.

Damages are not an adequate remedy

Specific performance is available only if damages are not an adequate remedy and it is for the claimant to establish that this is the case.

No substitute is available

The essence of breach of contract is that one party has failed to provide that which he was bound to provide. An award of damages will often enable the claimant to purchase that property or service from an alternative source; in other words, the party in breach will pay the injured party a sufficient sum to enable him to pay someone else to do that which the party in breach should have done. However, if there is no alternative source available – such as the purchase of 'one-off' goods – then damages are not adequate as no amount of money can purchase something which is simply not available.

KEY CASE

Cohen v Roche [1927] 1 KB 169

Concerning: availability of substitute goods

Facts

The claimant purchased eight Hepplewhite chairs at auction but the defendant refused to honour the sale as he claimed that there had been some irregularity in the transaction. The court held that the sale was valid but ordered an award of damages rather than the order of specific performance sought by the claimant.

Legal principle

It was held that the chairs were 'unremarkable' and possessed no special feature that made them unique and irreplaceable. As such, the claimant could obtain substitute chairs from another source and an order of specific performance would not be appropriate.

KEY CASE

Phillips v Lamdin [1949] 2 KB 33

Concerning: unavailability of substitute goods

Facts

The claimant agreed to purchase a house from the defendant which included a rare, ornate door made by Adam. The defendant delayed the sale of the house and removed the door prior to the completion of the sale.

Legal principle

It was held that the door could not be remade or refashioned – 'you cannot make a new Adam door' – thus it was not an option for the defendant to offer money to cover the value of the door but he must return it to its original position in the house.

The key feature to look out for here is whether the property in question is, if not entirely unique, of limited availability, as only then is it possible that an order of specific performance will be made to compel the party in breach to deliver the goods. Remember that the courts tend to view land as unique irrespective of its characteristics.

An award of damages would be unfair to the claimant

An award of damages would not be adequate if it would cause unfairness to the claimant, i.e. it would leave the claimant without adequate recompense. For example, if the financial value of the loss is very low, a successful claimant will receive only nominal damages, so this would not be an appropriate way of dealing with the case.

KEY CASE

Beswick v *Beswick* [1968] AC 58

Concerning: unfairness to the claimant

Facts

The claimant was the widow of a coal merchant who, prior to his death, had sold the goodwill in his business to the defendant on the agreement that the defendant would pay an annuity to the coal merchant during his lifetime and to his widow after his death. The defendant made one payment to the coal merchant and none to his widow. The claimant was not a party to the contract and so she could not sue for the unpaid annuity; instead she brought an action on behalf of her deceased husband's estate.

Legal principle

It would be unfair to the claimant to award damages as a remedy as these would only be nominal because the estate had suffered no loss as a *result* of the breach of contract, whereas an order of specific performance would compel the defendant to pay the unpaid sums and to continue to pay the annuity in the future.

Sale of Goods Act 1979, section 52

KEY STATUTE

Sale of Goods Act 1979, section 52(1)

In any action for breach of contract to deliver specific or ascertained goods the court may, if it thinks fit, on the plaintiff's [now claimant's] application, by its judgment or decree direct that the contract shall be performed specifically, without giving the defendant the option of retaining the goods on payment of damages.

This means that, if the goods are specific or ascertained, specific performance is available at the court's discretion. Despite this, in practice, the courts apply the common law 'availability of a substitute' rule to determine whether specific performance should be awarded.

Discretion of the court

As it is an equitable remedy, specific performance will be ordered only in accordance with the rules of equity; it was held in *Stickney* v *Keeble* [1915] AC 386 that 'equity will only grant specific performance if, under all the circumstances, it is just and equitable to do so'. An examination of case law identifies a number of principles that have been developed which guide the exercise of this discretion:

9 REMEDIES

- A claimant who delays in bringing an action may be denied specific performance: *Milward v Earl of Thanet* (1801) 5 Ves 720 (delay defeats equity).

- Specific performance is not available to a claimant who has behaved dishonestly or improperly: *Walters* v *Morgan* (1861) 2 Cox 369 (he who comes to equity must come with clean hands).

- A defendant may resist specific performance on the basis that it would cause extreme hardship to him: *Patel* v *Ali* [1984] 1 All ER 978.

- Specific performance will be refused if it is not possible for the defendant to perform what was agreed, i.e. if the property no longer belongs to the defendant.

- A claimant will not be granted specific performance where he has provided no consideration (equity will not assist a volunteer).

- Specific performance will be granted only if the claimant is also willing to perform his side of the bargain.

- Specific performance will not be ordered if the contract requires performance over a period of time so that constant supervision is needed as this would be impractical: *Co-operative Insurance Society Ltd* v *Argyll Stores (Holdings) Ltd* [1997] 3 All ER 297 (equity does nothing in vain).

KEY CASE

Co-operative Insurance Society Ltd v *Argyll Stores (Holdings) Ltd* **[1997] 3 All ER 297**

Concerning: constant supervision

Facts

The defendants operated a supermarket in a large unit that they leased in the claimants' retail centre. The lease had a covenant that required the supermarket to be open during normal business hours but it became unprofitable for the defendants and they ceased trading. The claimants feared that this would have an adverse impact on the level of trade in the retail centre, so they sought an order of specific performance to compel the defendants to re-open the supermarket and resume trading.

Legal principle

The House of Lords, overturning the ruling of the Court of Appeal, held that it was not practical for the courts to force the defendants to carry out their business as it would need constant supervision by the courts to ensure compliance. Moreover, given that the defendants ceased trading for economic reasons, specific performance would place them in the position of either having to trade an unprofitable business or pay damages to the court for contempt if they chose to defy the order of specific performance.

Type of contract

As a general rule, specific performance will not be ordered in relation to contracts for personal services, such as a contract of employment. Section 236 of the Trade Union and Labour Relations (Consolidation) Act 1992 states that it is unlawful to compel an employee to work by means of an order of specific performance or by grant of an injunction. Moreover, although an employment tribunal can order reinstatement or re-engagement of an employee who should not have been dismissed, it is rare for them to do so. There are pragmatic reasons for this position:

> Very rarely indeed will a court enforce . . . , a contract for services. The reason is obvious; if one party has no faith in the honesty, integrity or the loyalty of the other, to force him to serve or employ that other is a plain recipe for disaster.

 Make your answer stand out

Per Geoffrey Lane LJ in *Chappell* v *Times Newspapers Ltd* [1975] 1 WLR 482 at 506.

The relationship between damages and specific performance as remedies for breach of contract has been the subject of a fair amount of academic discussion. If you were required to evaluate the desirability of the availability of both remedies as part of an essay, familiarity with the academic debate would be useful. Bishop's (1985) article provides a detailed examination of this issue.

■ Putting it all together

Answer guidelines

See the sample question at the start of the chapter.

Approaching the question

This is an example of a problem question that requires a strong focus on damages. The instruction that accompanies the facts stipulates that you should advise Sally on the extent of her claim in damages. This means that there is no need to cover contract formation or breach of contract and that no credit would be available if you did include a discussion of these matters in your answer. Make sure you follow the instructions and that you identify each potential basis upon which damages could be awarded. ▶

Important points to include

- Start by picking out all of the areas where Sally has lost actual money or expected money as these provide a relatively straightforward basis upon which damages could be awarded. Once you have done this, look at the facts that remain and consider whether there is any non-pecuniary loss that could be reflected by an award of damages.

- The first issue to consider is whether Sally can recover damages for the loss of profit caused by the cancelled anniversary booking. Remember that you must establish that Alan's breach of contract (failing to finish the work in the time frame that was agreed) has caused this loss and that the damage is not too remote. Take the *Hadley* v *Baxendale* limbs into account here: was it in the ordinary course of things or was it within the contemplation of the parties at the time that the contract was made. Note that Sally made Alan aware about the booking after the contract was made but this could be countered by taking into account that he was engaged to install commercial catering equipment and that the time frame was stipulated at the start of the contract.

- Consider next whether Sally can recover damages for the loss of the executive lunches booking. Address issues of causation and remoteness again. Was this within the contemplation of the parties at the time that the contract was made? It could be argued that this is analogous to the government contracts in *Victoria Laundry* because Alan could not be expected to be aware of other plans that Sally had for seeking out bookings although there is a counter-argument that he must have been aware that she would be trying to generate business.

- Can Sally recover damages in relation to the mental distress that she suffered following the failure of her business? This is unlikely for two reasons, both of which should be explained in detail. First, *Addis* v *Gramophone Co Ltd* provides that damages for mental distress are not available in commercial contracts. Here, we know that Sally is having this work done as part of her new catering business and we can assume that Alan is undertaking the work as part of a commercial undertaking because payment has been agreed for his work. Second, damages for mental distress have been limited in cases such as *Jarvis* v *Swan Tours* to situations where enjoyment was the essential character of the contract, which is not the case here.

 Make your answer stand out

- A stronger answer to the question would incorporate a discussion of whether a claim of damages based upon reliance loss or one based on expectation loss (loss of bargain) would be most advantageous for Sally. A clear explanation of these two approaches and an application to the facts to demonstrate the difference in outcome would be sure to attract credit.

- Make sure that you can incorporate case law into your answer as this provides support for the principles that you have stated. It is always useful to find parallels between the facts of the problems and the facts of cases as this strengthens your argument as to how the law should be applied. For example, in this scenario, the loss of the anniversary booking and the loss of the lunch contract mirror the two bases of loss that were argued in *Victoria Laundry* so it would strengthen your answer to point this out.

READ TO IMPRESS

Bishop, W. (1985) The choice of remedy for breach of contract. *Legal Studies,* 14: 299.

Kramer, A. (2009) The new test of remoteness in contract. *Law Quarterly Review,* 125: 408.

Tettenborn, A. (2003) *Hadley* v *Baxendale* foreseeability: a principle beyond its sell-by date? *Journal of Contract Law,* 120.

www.pearsoned.co.uk/lawexpress

 Go online to access more revision support including quizzes to test your knowledge, sample questions with answer guidelines, podcasts you can download, and more!

And finally, before the exam . . .

By using this revision guide to direct your work, you should now have a good knowledge and understanding of the way in which the various aspects of the law of contract work in isolation and the many areas in which they overlap or are interrelated. You should also have brushed up the skills and techniques to demonstrate that knowledge and understanding in the examination, regardless of whether the questions are presented to you in essay or problem format.

Check your progress

☐ Look at the **revision checklists** at the start of each chapter. Are you happy that you can now tick them all? If not, go back to the particular chapter and work through the material again. If you are still struggling, seek help from your tutor.

☐ Attempt the **sample questions** in each chapter and check your answers against the guidelines provided.

☐ Go online to **www.pearsoned.co.uk/lawexpress** for more hands-on revision help:

  ☐ Try the **test your knowledge** quizzes and see if you can score full marks for each chapter.

  ☐ Attempt to answer the **sample questions** for each chapter within the time limit and check your answers against the guidelines provided.

  ☐ Listen to the **podcast** and then attempt the question it discusses.

  ☐ Evaluate sample exam answers in **you be the marker** and see if you can spot their strengths and weaknesses.

  ☐ Use the **flashcards** to test your recall of the legal principles of the key cases and statutes you've revised and the definitions of important terms.

■ Linking it all up

This book has provided a series of questions on contract law but you should remember that these topics can be combined to create questions that require knowledge of a whole range of different areas of contract law. Make sure that you cover as much of the syllabus as you can in your revision so that you can avoid the stressful situation of only being able to tackle part of a problem question.

Check where there are overlaps between subject areas. (You may want to review the 'revision note' boxes throughout this book.) Make a careful note of these, as knowing how one topic may lead into another can increase your marks significantly. Here are some examples:

✔ Questions on unfair contract terms or exclusion clauses (for example) will still require you to establish that a contract exists between the parties (involving offer, acceptance, consideration and intention to create legal relations).

✔ Almost any question involving a breach of contract could lead on to a discussion of contractual remedies.

✔ A breach of contract (or the setting aside of a contract) could arise for many possible reasons: for instance, misrepresentation, mistake, duress or undue influence.

■ Knowing your cases

Make sure you know how to use relevant case law in your answers. Use the table below to focus your revision of the key cases in each topic. To review the details of these cases, refer back to the particular chapter.

Key case	How to use	Related topics
Chapter 1 – Agreement and contractual intention		
Partridge v *Crittenden*	To show that an advertisement is an invitation to treat	Offer
Carlill v *Carbolic Smoke Ball Co*	To explain that unilateral offers can be made to the world at large and acceptance need not be communicated	Invitation to treat

Key case	How to use	Related topics
Chapter 1 – Agreement and contractual intention *Continued*		
Pharmaceutical Society of Great Britain v *Boots*	To show that the display of goods in a self-service shop is an invitation to treat	Offer
Fisher v *Bell*	To show that the display of goods in a shop window is an invitation to treat	Offer
British Car Auctions v *Wright*	To distinguish between offer, acceptance and invitation to treat at an auction sale	Offer, acceptance, invitation to treat
Harvey v *Facey*	To show that a statement of price is not an offer capable of acceptance	Offer and acceptance
Byrne v *Van Tienhoven*	To demonstrate that communication of revocation must be received	Offer, revocation
Errington v *Errington & Woods*	To demonstrate the revocation of a unilateral offer	Offer
Ramsgate Victoria Hotel v *Montefiore*	To show that offers can lapse after a reasonable time	Offer
Hyde v *Wrench*	To show that a counter offer will destroy an initial offer such that it may no longer be accepted	Offer and acceptance
Stevenson, Jacques & Co v *McLean*	To show that a request for information does not destroy an initial offer	Offer and acceptance
Felthouse v *Bindley*	To establish that silence can never constitute acceptance	

▶

Key case	How to use	Related topics
Chapter 1 – Agreement and contractual intention *Continued*		
Brogden v *Metropolitan Railway*	To show that acceptance can be inferred by conduct	
Adams v *Lindsell*	To set out the postal rule: that acceptance by post is made at the time the letter is posted	Offer and acceptance
Brinkibon v *Stahag Stahl*	To show that there is no single rule that covers acceptance by non-instantaneous communication	Offer and acceptance
Balfour v *Balfour*	To show that there is a contractually overrideable presumption that there is no intention to create legal relations between family members	
Chapter 2 – Consideration and promissory estoppel		
Currie v *Misa*	To provide the classic definition of consideration	
Dunlop v *Selfridge*	To provide a more sophisticated definition of consideration	
Tweddle v *Atkinson*	To show that a person can enforce a promise only if they have provided consideration themselves (it cannot move from a third party)	
Re McArdle	To show the general rule that consideration cannot be past	

Key case	How to use	Related topics
Chapter 2 – Consideration and promissory estoppel *Continued*		
Lampleigh v *Braithwaite*	To demonstrate an exception to the general rule that consideration cannot be past	
Thomas v *Thomas*	To show that consideration must be sufficient but need not be adequate	
Chappel v *Nestlé*	To show an example of apparently worthless items being good consideration	
Collins v *Godefroy*	To show that the performance of an existing public duty is not good consideration for a new promise	
Stilk v *Myrick*	To show that the performance of an existing contractual duty is not good consideration for a new promise	
Glassbrook Bros v *Glamorgan CC*	To demonstrate that exceeding an existing public duty can be good consideration for a new promise	
Hartley v *Ponsonby*	To demonstrate that exceeding an existing contractual duty can be good consideration for a new promise	

▶

Key case	How to use	Related topics
Chapter 2 – Consideration and promissory estoppel *Continued*		
Scotson v *Pegg*	To show that the performance of an existing contractual duty owed to a third party can be good consideration for a new promise	
Williams v *Roffey*	To show that conferring a 'practical benefit' can be good consideration for a new promise even where there is an existing contractual duty	
Pinnel's Case	To show that part payment of a debt can discharge the full debt if some additional consideration is provided	Promissory estoppel
Foakes v *Beer*	To demonstrate the potential harshness of the common law rule from *Pinnel's Case*	Promissory estoppel
Central London Property Trust v *High Trees House*	To demonstrate the equitable doctrine of promissory estoppel	Consideration
Chapter 3 – Contracts and third parties		
Dunlop v *Selfridge*	To set out the basic rule regarding privity of contract	Consideration
Shanklin Pier v *Detel Products*	To show how collateral contracts can avoid the rules relating to privity	Privity of contract

Key case	How to use	Related topics
Chapter 3 – Contracts and third parties *Continued*		
Tulk v *Moxhay*	To show how restrictive covenants can bind successive purchasers of land in equity without privity between them and the original seller	Privity of contract
Jackson v *Horizon Holidays*	To give an example of circumstances in which a third party was allowed to recover damages	
Woodar v *Wimpey*	To show how the House of Lords narrowed the rule from *Jackson* v *Horizon Holidays*	
Alfred McAlpine v *Panatown*	To demonstrate the application of the general principle that third parties should be allowed a remedy without privity (in the absence of no other remedy)	
Chapter 4 – Contractual terms		
J Evans and Son v *Mezario*	To show that contractual terms may be evidenced partly in writing, partly orally and partly by conduct	Incorporation of terms
L'Estrange v *Graucob*	To show that a party is generally bound by the terms of a signed agreement even if they have not read it	Incorporation of terms, Exclusion clauses

►

Key case	How to use	Related topics
Chapter 4 – Contractual terms *Continued*		
Bannerman v *White*	To show that the more important a pre-contractual statement, the more likely it is to be considered a term of the contract	Incorporation of terms
Dick Bentley Productions v *Harold Smith (Motors)*	To establish that pre-contractual statements made by parties with specialist knowledge can be considered terms of the contract	Incorporation of terms
Routledge v *McKay*	To show that where there is a considerable lapse of time between a pre-contractual statement and formation of the contract, the statement is likely to be a representation, not a term	Incorporation of terms
Poussard v *Spiers*	To illustrate that breach of a condition permits repudiation and termination of the contract	Warranties, innominate terms
Bettini v *Gye*	To show that breach of a warranty gives rise to an action in damages only and not repudiation	Conditions, innominate terms
Hong Kong Fir Shipping v *Kawasaki*	To show that the remedy for breach of an innominate term is decided once the effects of the breach are known	Conditions, warranties

Key case	How to use	Related topics
Chapter 4 – Contractual terms *Continued*		
The Moorcock	To illustrate that contractual terms may be implied by fact at common law	Officious bystander
Liverpool City Council v *Irwin*	To illustrate that contractual terms may be implied by law at common law	
Chapter 5 – Exclusion of liability		
L'Estrange v *Graucob*	To demonstrate incorporation of an exclusion clause by signature	Incorporation of terms
Curtis v *Chemical Cleaning*	To show that an exclusion clause in a signed contract can be wholly or partially invalidated by a misrepresentation as to its effect	Misrepresentation
Olley v *Marlborough Court Hotel*	To show that exclusion clauses must be introduced before or at the time of the contract	Incorporation of terms
Parker v *South Eastern Railway*	To show that a party who wishes to rely on an exclusion clause must take reasonable steps to bring it to the attention of the other party	Incorporation of terms

▶

Key case	How to use	Related topics
Chapter 5 – Exclusion of liability *Continued*		
Chapelton v *Barry Urban District Council*	To illustrate that an exclusion clause will only be incorporated if it is on a document that might reasonably be expected to contain contractual terms	Incorporation of terms
Thornton v *Shoe Lane Parking*	To demonstrate that a very high degree of notice is required for particularly onerous exclusion clauses to be effective	Incorporation of terms
The Mikhail Lermontov	To show that attention must be drawn to exclusion clauses that are incorporated by reference to another document	Incorporation of terms
Spurling v *Bradshaw*	To show that exclusion clauses can be incorporated by a regular course of dealings between the parties	Incorporation of terms
Houghton v *Trafalgar Insurance*	To give an example of the *contra proferentem* rule – the benefit of any doubt in the wording of an exclusion clause is given to the claimant	
Hollier v *Rambler Motors*	To show that exclusion clauses attempting to exclude negligence liability must be very clear and precise	
Photo Productions v *Securicor*	To show the rejection of the doctrine of fundamental breach	

AND FINALLY, BEFORE THE EXAM . . .

Key case	How to use	Related topics
Chapter 6 – Misrepresentation, mistake and illegality		
Bissett v *Wilkinson*	To establish that a false statement of opinion is not a misrepresentation of fact	
Dimmock v *Hallett*	To show that 'sales talk' is not a statement of fact	
Edgington v *Fitzmaurice*	To illustrate that an untrue statement of future intention can be a misrepresentation of fact	
Solle v *Butcher*	To show the distinction between false statements of law and false statements of fact	
Keates v *Cadogan*	To show the general rule that silence cannot amount to misrepresentation	
With v *O'Flanagan*	To show that there is a positive obligation to disclose changes to statements that were true at the time of making them but which subsequently become untrue	
Spice Girls v *Aprilia*	To demonstrate that a misrepresentation can be made by conduct	
Horsefall v *Thomas*	To show that the claimant must be aware of the misrepresentation	
Attwood v *Small*	To show that the claimant must have relied upon the misrepresentation	

▶

Key case	How to use	Related topics
Chapter 6 – Misrepresentation, mistake and illegality *Continued*		
JEB Fasteners v *Marks Bloom*	To show that reliance may also be shown by acting upon the misrepresentation	
Derry v *Peek*	To set out the requirements for fraudulent misrepresentation	
Hedley Byrne v *Heller*	To show that damages may be recoverable at common law for negligent misstatement that causes financial loss	
Esso Petroleum v *Marden*	To show that negligent misstatement can include representations as to a future state of affairs	
Salt v *Stratstone Specialist*	To illustrate that recission should be an available remedy for misrepresentation if 'practical justice' can be done	
Couturier v *Hastie*	To illustrate *res extincta* as a type of common mistake	
Cooper v *Phibbs*	To illustrate *res sua* as a type of common mistake	
Bell v *Lever Brothers*	To illustrate mistake as to quality as a type of common mistake	
Raffles v *Wichelhaus*	To illustrate mutual mistake as to the terms of the contract	
Scriven Brothers v *Hindley*	To illustrate mutual mistake as to the subject matter of the contract	

Key case	How to use	Related topics
Chapter 6 – Misrepresentation, mistake and illegality *Continued*		
Hartog v *Colin & Shields*	To illustrate the operation of unilateral mistake as to the terms of the contract	
Chapter 7 – Duress and undue influence		
Barton v *Armstrong*	To show that actual or threatened violence will amount to duress	
The Atlantic Baron	To demonstrate that duress may also arise by economic pressure	
Pao On v *Lau Yiu Long*	To set out the requirements of economic duress	
The Universal Sentinel	To illustrate the view that the test for duress should consider whether the innocent party was given any practical alternative other than compliance	
Williams v *Bayley*	To demonstrate the operation of actual undue influence	
RBS v *Etridge (No. 2)*	To set out the rules on constructive notice which apply where a wife claims her consent was obtained by the undue influence of her husband	
Cheese v *Thomas*	To give an example of how remedies may be ineffective where the value of the property has changed	Undue influence

▶

Key case	How to use	Related topics
Chapter 8 – Discharge of a contract		
Cutter v *Powell*	To exemplify the potentially harsh outcome of the strict rule of discharge by performance	
Re Moore & Co's Arbitration	To exemplify the potentially harsh outcome of the strict rule of discharge by performance in relation to sale of goods	
Roberts v *Havelock*	To demonstrate that partly performed severable contracts can be enforced	
Sumpter v *Hedges*	To show that partial performance is only enforceable where the defendant has free choice whether or not to accept that partial performance	
Dakin v *Lee*	To show that substantial performance can render a contract enforceable subject to damages in respect of that which is incomplete	
Bolton v *Mahadeva*	To give an example of the difficulty in determining what constitutes 'substantial' performance	
Startup v *MacDonald*	To show that tender of performance can be equivalent to performance	
Paradine v *Jane*	To show the historical absolute nature of contractual obligations	

Key case	How to use	Related topics
Chapter 8 – Discharge of a contract *Continued*		
Krell v *Henry*	To show that contracts may be frustrated where an event destroys the central purpose of the contract	
Herne Bay Steamboat v *Hutton*	To show that contracts are not frustrated where there is some commercial purpose left in the contract	
Chandler v *Webster*	To demonstrate the effect of frustration at common law	
Fibrosa v *Fairbairn*	To set out the modified common law rule on frustration where there is a total failure of consideration	
Chapter 9 – Remedies		
County v *Girozentrale*	To demonstrate a break in the chain of causation	
Hadley v *Baxendale*	To set out the two key tests for remoteness in damages	
Victoria Laundry v *Newman*	To illustrate recovery of losses within the contemplation of the parties and set out the test as 'reasonable foreseeability'	Remoteness
The Heron II	To illustrate recovery of losses within the contemplation of the parties and set out the test as 'not unlikely'	Remoteness

▶

Key case	How to use	Related topics
Chapter 9 – Remedies *Continued*		
Brace v *Calder*	To show the duty to take reasonable steps to mitigate losses arising from a breach of contract	
Pilkington v *Wood*	To show there is no duty to take onerous steps to mitigate losses arising from a breach of contract	
Ruxley Electronics v *Forsyth*	To show that an award of contractual damages does not necessarily mean awarding the monetary equivalent of specific performance	
Attorney General v *Blake*	To show that the courts can exceptionally award an account of profits arising from a breach of contract	
Anglia Television v *Reed*	To show the operation of reliance loss: putting the innocent party in the position they would have been in had the contract never been made	
Jarvis v *Swans Tours*	To give an example of damages being awarded for loss of enjoyment	
Cohen v *Roche*	To show that orders of specific performance are not appropriate where substitute goods are available	

Key case	How to use	Related topics
Chapter 9 – Remedies *Continued*		
Phillips v *Lamdin*	To show that orders of specific performance are appropriate where substitute goods are not available	
Beswick v *Beswick*	To show that specific performance can be a preferable remedy where an award of damages would be unfair to the claimant	
Co-operative Insurance v *Argyll Stores*	To show that specific performance will not be ordered in cases where constant supervision would be required	

■ Sample question

Below is a problem question that incorporates overlapping areas of the law. See if you can answer this question drawing upon your knowledge of the whole subject area. Guidelines on answering this question are included at the end of this section.

PROBLEM QUESTION

Jerry wanted to buy a moped for his teenage daughter, Heather. They visited the local second-hand moped dealer, 'Federico's Italian Scooters'. They saw a two-year-old pink moped, which was just what Heather wanted. Jerry asked the sales manager, Tina, whether the scooter was reliable. Tina told him: 'It's a great little runner.' Jerry also asked whether it had ever been involved in an accident, to which Tina replied: 'Not that I know of.' Jerry was happy, so he paid £1,250 for the scooter.

That evening, Heather took the scooter out to go to her saxophone lesson. As she tried to stop at a junction, the brakes seized and she fell off. Fortunately, she was not hurt, ▶

but her new designer 'Snugg' boots were badly scuffed and her saxophone was dented. Her saxophone teacher also charged Jerry for the cost of the missed lesson. A friend of Jerry's (who is a professional mechanic) examined the scooter and told Jerry that the brakes must have been defective for some time. He also discovered that the suspension brackets had been repaired and rewelded. It looked like the moped had been in a separate accident some time before Heather's.

Jerry took the moped back to the dealer. Tina was unhelpful. She pointed to a sign on the counter which said 'Federico's accepts no liability for defects in any goods sold' and told Jerry that he could not have his money back.

Advise Jerry and Heather whether they have any claims against Federico's Italian Scooters in contract and what damages (if any) they may recover if successful.

Answer guidelines

Approaching the question

This question raises several issues and illustrates how various parts of the course can be linked together quite readily. In a complex problem situation like this, you must take time to consider the facts carefully and work out the order in which you are going to attack them. Here you are specifically asked to advise Jerry and Heather, so you should start by working out exactly what has happened to them and the circumstances of each potential basis for a claim.

Important points to include

Tina's statements

- Are these actionable misrepresentations? Requires statement of material fact made prior to the contract made by one party to the contract which is false or misleading and which induced the other party to enter into the contract.

- Tina made two representations. First, that the moped was a 'great little runner'. Is this a mere sales puff (*Dimmock* v *Hallett*)? Second, she said that the moped had not been in an accident as far as she knew. While there is no general duty to disclose material facts (*Keates* v *Cadogan*), there may be the deliberate covering up of a defect (*Sybron Corporation* v *Rochem*). Perhaps Tina's lack of awareness was a result of having failed to make due enquiry (*Notts Patent Brick and Tile Co* v *Butler*)?

- The representations were made prior to the contract and must also have materially affected Jerry's judgement so that he was induced by it or acted in reliance upon it.

It is unlikely that Jerry would have bought the moped if Tina had said it had problems and had actually been repaired following a prior accident.

- Remedies for misrepresentation depend on the type of misrepresentation: innocent or negligent misrepresentation gives rise to rescission and/or damages; fraudulent misrepresentation can give rise to rescission or damages. The status of Tina's misrepresentations will depend on her knowledge at the time of making them.

Jerry's contract

- Jerry has a contract with Federico's for the sale of the moped. There is offer and acceptance, consideration (£1,250) and intention to create legal relations can be presumed since this is a business-to-consumer transaction.

- Since this is a contract for the sale of goods in the course of a business, certain terms are implied by the Sale of Goods Act (SGA) 1979 – particularly section 14(2) relating to quality (which is further defined in section 14(2A) and (2B)).

- The moped is probably not of satisfactory quality (defective brakes) and thus there is likely to be a breach of the term implied into the contract by section 9(3)(d) CRA (safety).

- Federico's attempts to rely on the exclusion clause. At common law, terms incorporated by notice must be introduced before or at the time of the contract (*Olley* v *Marlborough Court Hotel*) and the party subject to the clause must be made sufficiently aware of its existence (*Parker* v *South Eastern Railway*). While the sign is at the counter, it is not clear how prominently it was displayed or whether Jerry knew about it before entering into the contract.

- If the term is incorporated, it will be necessary to consider the CRA further. Notices must be fair (section 62) and transparent (section 68). The notice is certainly plain and intelligible. Was it legible? In any case, it appears to create a significance imbalance to Jerry's detriment, so it is therefore highly unlikely that Federico's will be able to rely upon it and thus will be liable to Jerry for breach of contract.

- Jerry will be able to recover damages for losses arising naturally from the breach of contract (the loss of the moped) and that which was reasonably within the contemplation of the parties at the time that the contract was formed (*Hadley* v *Baxendale*; *Victoria Laundry*; *Heron II*).

Heather's losses

- Heather is not a party to the contract for the sale of the moped. Generally, only parties to a contract can acquire rights and liabilities under it (*Dunlop* v *Selfridge*).

- This is not a situation which appears to fall within any of the statutory exceptions.

It also appears that the Contracts (Rights of Third Parties) Act 1999 will be unable to assist Heather.

▶

Make your answer stand out

Good, logical and methodical structure is key to success in a question like this. Many answers to questions which raise different legal issues are characterised by often chaotic responses which attempt to deal with multiple issues all at once. Once you have identified the potential heads of claim, deal with each of them individually and thoroughly before moving on to the next. The ability to construct a clear line of legally reasoned argument is crucial.

Further practice

To test yourself further, try to answer these three questions, which also incorporate overlapping areas of the law. Evaluate your answers using the answer guidelines available on the companion website at **www.pearsoned.co.uk/lawexpress**

Question 1

Mr Khan runs a very successful Indian takeaway. He has been trading for over 20 years and has a large and loyal customer base. After much lobbying from his customers, he decided to expand his premises to incorporate a restaurant area in addition to his takeaway business. Four months ago, Mr Khan bought the coffee shop next door to his takeaway. He then entered into a contract with Boyer's Buildings Limited to knock through and convert the former coffee shop into the new restaurant area for a total cost of £30,000. Works were agreed to commence on 17 September and were estimated to take around six weeks. Mr Khan agreed to pay 20% of the contract price on commencement, with a further 30% after three weeks and the final 50% on completion. Boyer's Buildings commenced work on the agreed date.

Consider the following three separate scenarios. Advise Mr Khan on each.

(a) Two weeks into the job, their project manager, Wayne, sent Mr Khan an email. It read:

> Really sorry about this, but I've underestimated the materials needed for the conversion. It's putting us back a bit as I don't have the cash to buy the extra. It will probably mean we take about eight weeks rather than six. Hope that won't be a problem. Cheers, Wayne

Mr Khan had already sent out a load of leaflets announcing his Grand Opening to coincide with Bonfire Night and had already been taking bookings for the restaurant. He said that he would pay Boyer's Buildings an extra £5,000 if they guaranteed that the work would be done by the end of October. Wayne agreed.

The work was finished on time. Mr Khan paid the second and completion instalments under the existing contract. He now says that he should not need to pay the extra £5,000 as Boyer's Buildings did what they said they were going to do in the first place.

(b) Four weeks into the job, their project manager, Wayne, sent Mr Khan an email. It read:

> Really sorry about this, but we've still got loads of work on renovating that old house. You know, the one where that regular customer of yours lives? Anyway, there's no way we're going to be able to finish yours, so cheers and that for paying up to date, but we're pulling off site tomorrow.

Mr Khan found another builder who finished the job on time, but charged him £25,000 for doing so.

(c) Mr Khan is worried that the work that Boyer's Buildings is doing at the restaurant is shoddy. After two weeks, Mr Khan told their project manager, Wayne, that he wanted him to stop work so he could find an alternative builder to complete the job on time. When Wayne went to work the next day, he found that Mr Khan had changed the locks on the former coffee shop and he could not gain access to continue with construction.

Question 2

'English law on contract has generally developed on the basis of the principle that the parties to a contract are free to include within in it any terms that they wish. However, significant exceptions to this general principle have developed over the years in order to address situations where the inequalities of bargaining power between the parties would lead to an unjust contract.'

Discuss.

Question 3

In July 2014, Amber rented her mobile home to Grant for £85 per week for three years. Grant was studying law at university and had decided to live in the mobile home during term time. His Aunt Dorothy also lent him £800 to buy furniture for the mobile home to be paid back within the following year.

However, in March 2015, Grant suffered a nervous breakdown brought on by the sheer volume of work and was unable to study. When Amber heard about this she agreed to accept 'half rent until you make a full recovery'. Aunt Dorothy was equally sympathetic and agreed that the £250 that Grant had already paid her back would suffice. She said he could 'forget about the rest'.

Since then Grant has paid £50 per week in rent to Amber. In September 2015, Grant decided that his health would no longer permit him to continue his studies and he dropped out of university.

He is now unemployed but, last week, Amber discovered that Grant had just won £1 million on the Euromillions lottery.

Advise Grant.

Glossary of terms

The glossary is divided into two parts: key definitions and other useful terms. The key definitions can be found within the chapter in which they occur as well as in the glossary below. These definitions are the essential terms that you must know and understand in order to prepare for an exam. The additional list of terms provides further definitions of useful terms and phrases that will also help you answer examination and coursework questions effectively. These terms are highlighted in the text as they occur but the definition can only be found here.

■ Key definitions

Acceptance	Final and unqualified expression of assent to the terms of an offer.
Actionable misrepresentation	A statement of material fact made prior to the contract by one party to the contract to the other which is false or misleading and which induced the other party to enter into the contract.
Battle of the forms	The situation that arises where one or both of the parties attempt to rely on their standard terms is often referred to as the 'battle of the forms'.
Breach of contract	Committed when a party without lawful excuse fails or refuses to perform what is due from them under the contract, or performs defectively or incapacitates themselves from performing.
Damages	A financial remedy that aims to compensate the injured party for the consequences of the breach of contract.
Doctrine of frustration	Under the doctrine of frustration a contract may be discharged if, after its formation, events occur making its performance impossible or illegal and in certain analogous situations.

Duty to mitigate	Principle of contract law whereby the innocent party who has suffered a breach of contract has a duty to take reasonable steps to minimise the extent of their loss arising from the breach.
Invitation to treat	A preliminary statement expressing a willingness to receive offers.
Mirror image rule	The principle that a valid acceptance must correspond exactly with the terms of the offer is sometimes referred to as the 'mirror image rule'.
Offer	An expression of willingness to contract on specified terms, made with the intention that it is to become binding as soon as it is accepted by the person to whom it is addressed.
Offeree	The party to whom an offer is addressed.
Offeror	The party who makes an offer.
Puff	A boastful statement made in advertising.
Representation	A statement which induces a party to enter into a contract (but does not form part of it).
Revocation	The rescinding, annulling or withdrawal of an offer.
Severable obligations	A contract imposes severable obligations if payment under it is due from time to time as performance of a specified part of the contract is rendered.
Specific performance	An equitable remedy that compels the party in breach to perform his part of the contract.
Term	A promise or undertaking which becomes part of the contract itself.
Unilateral offer	An offer where one party promises to pay the other a sum of money (or to do some other act) if the other will do something (or forbear from doing so) without making any promise to that effect.

■ Other useful terms

Agent	The agent is a party to the contract with the third party. The agent has a direct contractual relationship with the third party, but makes the contract on behalf of the principal and not on his own behalf.

Bilateral contract	A contract in which each party undertakes an obligation.
Common mistake	A category of mistake in which both parties make the same mistake.
Condition	A key term in a contract. If breached, the injured party can repudiate the contract.
Consideration	Consideration is an act or promise of forbearance which 'buys' the promise of the other party. Consideration renders a promise enforceable in law.
Innominate term	Term where the court looks at the effects of the breach on the injured party to determine whether the breach itself was of a condition or a warranty.
Mitigation of loss	A duty to keep one's losses to a minimum.
Mutual mistake	A category of mistake where the parties are at cross-purposes, but each believes that the other is in agreement.
Principal	The party on whose behalf a contract is made and who receives the benefit arising under the contract.
Quantum meruit	'As much as is deserved.' If a price has not been specified in a contract but work has been done or goods supplied under it, a quantum meruit action allows a claim for a reasonable price for the performance rendered.
Repudiation	Rejection of the continued existence of a contract.
Third party	The third party enters into the contract with the agent. However, the rules of agency provide that there is no contractual relationship with the agent. Instead the principal is bound by the contractual relationship with the third party which has been entered into by the agent on his behalf.
Uberrimae fidei	'Of utmost good faith.' Essential for the validity of certain contracts between parties with a particular relationship between them, such as contracts of insurance.
Unilateral contract	A contract in which only one party undertakes an obligation.
Unilateral mistake	A category of mistake where one party is mistaken and the other knows and takes advantage of the mistake.

Void contract

A contract which is treated as though it never existed so that it may be enforced by neither party.

Voidable contract

A contract in which the injured party can choose whether or not to be bound by it.

Warranty

A less important term in a contract. If breached, the injured party may sue for damages but is not entitled to repudiate the contract.

Index

LEARNING RESOURCE CENTRE
ASHFORD COLLEGE
JEMMETT ROAD
ASHFORD TN23 4RJ